HEDGING WITH FINANCIAL FUTURES FOR INSTITUTIONAL INVESTORS

HEDGING WITH FINANCIAL FUTURES FOR INSTITUTIONAL INVESTORS
From Theory to Practice

by
Stephen Figlewski

in collaboration with
Kose John *and*
John Merrick

Ballinger Publishing Company
Cambridge, Massachusetts
A Subsidiary of Harper & Row, Publishers, Inc.

International Standard Book Number: 0-88730-083-9

Library of Congress Catalog Card Number: 85-15782

Printed in the United States of America

Library of Congress Cataloging in Publication Data

Figlewski, Stephen.
 Hedging with financial futures for institutional investors.

 Includes index.
 1. Financial futures. 2. Hedging (Finance).
I. John, Kose. II. Merrick, John, 1954–
III. Title.
HG6024.3.F54   1985   332.64′5   85-15782
ISBN 0-88730-083-9

CONTENTS

LIST OF FIGURES

LIST OF TABLES

ACKNOWLEDGMENTS

Any major work such as this depends on the support, assistance, and interest of many people, only a few of whom can be acknowledged formally.

First of all, we would like to thank the American Council of Life Insurance for providing the financial support that made this project possible, and especially Kenneth Wright whose constant encouragement helped to keep things (more or less) on schedule. Arnold Sametz was also instrumental in setting the project up and helping to keep it running smoothly.

We are very grateful to the Interactive Data Corporation for providing nearly all of the data used in the empirical work, and to John Young for his able, and cheerful, research assistance in helping to put the data into shape.

A number of people read earlier drafts and generally provided very helpful comments both on style and on substance. We would especially like to thank David Dunford, Stan Jonas, Herbert Mann, Patricia Owens, Eliot Rosenthal, and William Silber, as well as the others, too numerous to name, who contributed important facts and insights during the course of the research.

Finally, we would like to thank Will Jones and Mary Jaffier for their patient efforts in typing the manuscript, and especially in setting, and resetting, the equations.

INTRODUCTION

The past several years have witnessed remarkable growth in financial futures markets. With the introduction of futures contracts on financial instruments, institutional investors now have the ability to use the futures markets to manage the financial risks in their business in the same way that hedgers in agricultural commodities have used commodity futures in the past. Proper use of financial futures can greatly extend the possibilities for risk management for a financial institution such as a life insurance company. But optimal use requires understanding of how futures contracts work, how to balance risk and return in a hedged position, and how to implement the hedging strategies that futures trading makes possible.

Many institutions regularly trade in volatile markets and hold large portfolios of securities that are susceptible to wide price swings, but have been slow to take advantage of the opportunity to hedge their risks with financial futures. This has in large part been due to a combination of legal restraints, such as state laws and regulations preventing the use of futures, and general caution about getting involved in markets that are perceived as being risky without a firm understanding of how they work.

As financial futures markets have developed and become more established and as greater volatility in financial markets has increased the need for better methods of controlling risk, the first of these barriers to the use of futures is beginning to be lifted. Laws preventing futures trading by life insurance companies have recently been liberalized in a number of key states, including New York, Connecticut, and Illinois, and the direction of change elsewhere is toward increased permissiveness in this area. The second hurdle — reluctance to enter markets and engage in hedging strategies that are not fully understood — is perhaps harder to overcome. The purpose of this book is to help reduce the cause of this reluctance.

This is the second of two documents that have been written under a grant from the American Council of Life Insurance to the Salomon Center for the Study of Financial Institutions at New York University Graduate School of Business Administration. The objective of the research funded by this grant has been to produce the kind of information that a financial institution will need to undertake a hedging program involving financial futures. The first document, *An Introduction to Financial Futures* by John Merrick and Stephen Figlewski, provides an overview of the financial futures markets. It was designed as a brief introduction to the concepts of futures trading and the ways that futures may be used in risk management, to be read fairly quickly by someone such as a senior investment manager who was already familiar with other financial markets but had no background in futures. This book will give a more detailed and technical approach to the subject, focusing on the design of risk management strategies and the operational details of implementing them. It is designed to be read and used as a reference by those in an operations or research capacity who will have the responsibility of setting up and running a futures hedging program. While we concentrate particularly on the markets and strategies that will be of most use to a life insurance company, we expect this material to be of widespread interest to institutional investors in general.

There are a number of books on futures markets, and financial futures in particular. Many are very well written and informative, and we recommend that those who will have operational responsibility for futures trading should read widely in the area before getting started. No single book can cover every topic completely, and different authors take different approaches, so a financial institution may well find one more suited to its needs than another.

There do, however, appear to be two basic orientations in existing futures markets literature. There are works targeted for traders and users of futures markets. These tend to be readable but generally not sufficiently detailed or accurate regarding the correct design and implementation of hedging strategies. Then there are works written more for the academic audience. These cover theoretical aspects of futures in rigorous detail but generally neglect the practical side of the markets that is needed to translate theory into practice.

This book is called *Hedging with Financial Futures for Institutional Investors: From Theory to Practice* to emphasize that our objective is to bridge the two approaches. What we try to do is to present the theory of hedging with financial futures in a way that is accurate and sufficiently detailed so that it may be incorporated into operational hedging strategies and yet is accessible to the nonacademic investment manager.

To promote understanding of the principles of futures, we devote considerable attention to a theoretical treatment of the basic questions in futures hedging. How does a futures hedge alter the risk and return of an investment? How should it be set up optimally? What types of strategies are possible, and which are most likely to be effective? However, at all times we want to keep in mind that the ultimate goal is successful application of the theory to actual risk management problems faced by institutional investors. To link theory to practice, we use numerous examples to illustrate specific points, usually based on actual market prices from recent years.

We also examine several larger case studies in depth, to show how all of the pieces fit together. These cases illustrate the implementation of hedge strategies as they might have been set up as of the beginning of 1984. We take data from the previous year and a half to estimate the appropriate hedge ratios and then examine the performance of the hedge strategies by month during the first ten months of 1984. This procedure gives a much clearer picture of how a given strategy performs than do examples involving only one-time hedges. The essential feature of a hedge is that it changes risk, but since risk is variability in the outcome from one time to the next, in order to see the true effect of a hedge on risk it is necessary to look at more than one trial.

The book will not be easy reading for a first-time user of futures markets, especially if his math skills are a little rusty. However, no math beyond algebra is used, so none of the material should be beyond the ability of a diligent reader. In a few sections we cover material at a more advanced level, which is not strictly essential for a first reading. These sections are marked with an (A) to indicate that they can be safely skipped by a reader with less interest in the area.

We begin in Chapter 1 with a review of investment mathematics for financial futures traders. In the same way that understanding bond yield calculations is essential in running a fixed income portfolio, understanding the mathematics of hedging is necessary to a successful use of the futures markets. We review the concepts of mean or expected returns, standard deviation, and correlation that will be used throughout the book. In this chapter we also discuss how these parameters should, and should not, be estimated from historical data.

Chapter 2 is concerned with the effect of a futures hedge on risk. Financial futures greatly increase the scope of risk management by allowing the investor to choose from a range of risk and return combinations simply by adjusting the hedge ratio. The main focus in this chapter is on determining the hedge ratio (i.e., the size of the futures position taken), which yields the minimum level of risk in the hedged position. We then discuss the kinds of risk, notably basis risk, that can not be eliminated in a futures hedge.

Risk reduction is only half of the story in hedging, since trading futures also alters expected returns. In Chapter 3 we discuss how a financial futures price is related to the price for the underlying asset by the "cost of carry" model. The difference between the futures price and the value of the item being hedged is known as the "basis," and how the basis changes over time determines both the risk and the return on a hedged position.

The first three chapters provide the necessary tools to design a hedge for a fixed-income portfolio. Chapter 4 applies them in two detailed examples. In the first, we set up and analyze a hedge of a portfolio of Treasury bonds using Treasury bond futures. The second example, involving more basis risk, concerns a hedge of a position in a single corporate bond.

Chapter 5 presents another important strategy involving futures on fixed-income securities: immunization. Financial futures can be used to alter the duration of a fixed-income portfolio easily in order to match a desired horizon. We describe a basic duration matching strategy and illustrate its use in a case where an insurance company writes a five-year guaranteed interest contract (GIC) and invests the proceeds in long-term bonds. A futures hedge is used to reduce the duration of the bond portfolio to match the GIC liability.

The most rapidly growing financial futures are those on stock indexes. Stock index futures add an important new dimension to investment management in equity portfolios, but they are somewhat less intuitive to apply than those on fixed-income securities since nearly every use involves a cross-hedge. Chapter 6 describes the concept and uses of stock index futures contracts and illustrates a variety of risk management strategies that are possible with this versatile instrument.

The preceding chapters covered the design of hedging strategies. In Chapter 7, we discuss topics relevant for the practical aspect of managing a hedge. These include selecting a futures commissions merchant, putting on a hedge, carrying a position and meeting margin calls, rolling over futures contracts as near months expire, and delivery.

1 REVIEW OF INVESTMENT MATHEMATICS FOR FUTURES TRADERS

The essence of hedging with financial futures is that the futures position taken combines with the existing cash market position to yield a desired exposure to risk on the overall investment. In order to do this optimally, or even to understand how risk and return change when futures are traded, a certain amount of mathematical analysis is required. This chapter will review the basic mathematics that will be employed throughout the book. We also cover pricing conventions used for several important cash market instruments and discuss procedures for estimating the parameters needed to design a hedge.

As a matter of terminology, we will regularly use the term "cash" security or "cash" market in its futures sense to refer to the item being hedged or the market in which it is traded. There is no direct connection to the instruments of the money market. A thirty-year bond will be called the cash security if it is what is being hedged. Another term with the same meaning is "spot," as in "the spot market."

The two essential elements of a hedged position are its expected return and its risk. Investors naturally want to maximize returns and minimize risk. Using the futures market allows them to alter both, but not independently; except under abnormal circumstances, reducing risk will also require giving up some expected return. We will start with a discussion of returns and then consider risk.

CALCULATING YIELDS

There are many different ways of measuring the "yield" of an investment. For a coupon-paying bond, there are coupon yield, current yield, yield to maturity, and holding period yield. For a stock, one might look at dividend yield, capital appreciation, and total return. Even in the case of a single payment instrument like a Treasury bill, yields are quoted both on discount basis and as a bond equivalent.

The yield concept most relevant to our discussion is holding period yield. Throughout the book we will focus on hedging assets that require a single investment at the beginning of the holding period and which generate one or more cash inflows during the period. This covers bonds, loans, and other fixed-income securities as well as stocks. Extending the analysis to liabilities of the same type (e.g., issuing a bond) is straightforward.

The simplest case is a security that will pay no coupon interest or dividend during the holding period — for example, a Treasury bill. Then

$$R = \frac{P_T - P_0}{P_0}, \tag{1.1}$$

where R is the holding period yield expressed as a decimal (e.g., 0.10 is 10%),

P_0 is the price at the beginning of the holding period, and

P_T is the price at the end of the holding period.

Example: At the 25 March 1985 Treasury bill auction, the average price paid for the three-month T-bill was 97.874. The ninety-one-day bill pays its face value of 100 at maturity, making its holding period yield

$$R = \frac{100 - 97.874}{97.874} = 0.0217 = 2.17\%.$$

One difficulty with this formulation is that the yield does not adjust for the length of the holding period. To make comparisons between investments held for different lengths of time, one typically annualizes the yield. This is done in one of two ways, either as simple interest (by multiplying R by the number of holding periods in a year) or by compounding. For simple interest

$$R_{\text{simple}} = n \times R, \tag{1.2}$$

where n is the number of periods in a year and R is the holding period yield from equation (1.1).

The compounded rate is given by

$$R_{\text{compound}} = (1+R)^n - 1. \tag{1.3}$$

Example: The T-bill in the last example has an annualized yield, calculated as simple interest, of

$$\frac{365}{91}(2.17) = 8.70\%.$$

The compounded annual yield is

$$(1.0217)^{365/91} - 1 = 1.0899 - 1 = 0.0899 = 8.99\%.$$

These two ways of annualizing yields naturally give different answers. The simple interest yield is less than the compound rate for periods less than one year and greater for longer periods, with the discrepancy being larger the higher is R.

Example: Suppose P_0 is 1.0 and P_T is 1.25. R is then 0.25 or 25%. If the holding period is six months, then

$$R_{\text{simple}} = (2)(0.25) = 0.50 = 50\%$$

$$R_{\text{compound}} = (1.25)^2 - 1 = 0.5625 = 56.25\%.$$

On the other hand, if the holding period is two years, then

$$R_{\text{simple}} = (1/2)(0.25) = 0.125 = 12.5\%$$

$$R_{\text{compound}} = (1.25)^{1/2} - 1 = 0.118 = 11.80\%.$$

Oddly, it is common practice to use simple interest in annualizing yields for holding periods less than a year and compound interest for longer periods.

For exactness it is normally most appropriate to use compound yields at all times, since this takes account of the fact that at the end of the holding period both principal and interest will be available to be reinvested. However, this can give rise to several problems. First, it does not correspond to the yield conventions widely in use among market participants. Second, it can potentially cause misleading results in annualizing fluctuating yields from very short holding periods. For example, it is not uncommon for a stock's price to change by 2 percent in a day. This corresponds to a compounded annualized return of $(1.02)^{365} - 1$ or 137,641 percent! Not surprisingly, a number of this size would dominate any calculation it was used in, more so than the annualized simple interest of 730 percent. The problem, of course, is that while a stock might go up 2 percent in one day, it is inconceivable that it could do so every day for a year.

The third problem is that compounding is more complicated than computing simple interest, and it often does not seem worth the bother to avoid small inexactitude. Whether compounding is really necessary depends to a large extent on the purpose of the yield calculation. If a computer program is being written to examine investment strategies in close detail, then compounding is very likely to be worth doing. On the other hand, if one is computing yields in order to compare two alternative investments, the important thing is that the return be computed by the same method for each — the *difference* in yields between them will generally be affected only minimally by the approximations that are commonly in use in the financial community.

Continuous Compounding (A)

These examples illustrate one problem of annualizing rates from very short holding periods: It is often necessary to take numbers to high or fractional powers. For example, an overnight investment such as a repurchase agreement is rolled over daily. If R is the one-day return, its annualized value is $(1+R)^{365} - 1$. An easy way to approximate such a calculation is to use *continuous* compounding. The important relationship is that, for R close to zero,

$$(1+R)^n \approx e^{nR}.$$

e represents the base of natural logarithms, about 2.7183, and the symbol $\approx$ means "is approximately equal to."

Example: A repurchase agreement that pays a daily rate of 0.00027 (2.7 basis points) has an annual rate, approximated by continuous compounding, of $e^{365(0.00027)} - 1 = e^{0.09855} - 1 = 0.1036 = 10.36\%$.

When R is expressed as an annual rate, one plus the return over any period of length T (measured in years and fractions, like $0.25 = 3$ months) is e^{RT}.

While continuous compounding can simplify many calculations involving short holding periods and daily interest, one must take care that the annual interest rate used is consistent with continuous compounding over the holding period. For example, the continuously compounded yield on a security that returns 10 percent over a six-month holding period is found as follows:

$$e^{R(0.5)} = 1.10$$

$$R = \frac{\log(1.10)}{0.5} = 19.1\%.$$

Money Market Yield Conventions (A)

Money market securities often use yield conventions involving inaccuracies beyond simple interest. Most are based on a 360-day year, and some such as Treasury bills are quoted on a "banker's discount" basis, with interest on a security that is sold at a discount taken as a percent of its par value. The T-bill yield expressed this way is given by

$$R_{\text{discount}} = \frac{360}{T}(100 - P_0), \tag{1.4}$$

where T is the maturity in days of the bill.

The T-bill yield computed in the earlier example corresponds to the "bond equivalent" T-bill rate, given by (1.5):

$$R_{\text{bond equivalent}} = R = \frac{365}{T}\left(\frac{100 - P_0}{P_0}\right) \times 100. \tag{1.5}$$

Commercial paper is also a discounted instrument and is quoted on a discount basis as given in equation (1.4). Eurodollar deposits and repurchase agreements are treated as interest-bearing securities, with the initial purchase price considered to be the principal amount on which interest is paid. However, a 360-day year is used in computing the interest payment. Thus the interest paid at maturity on a T-day term repurchase agreement with a stated rate of interest R is $(T/360)R$ per dollar initially invested. Large denomination bank certificates of deposit exist in both forms.

The only solution to this situation is that the analyst must know how yields are quoted on the instruments he is dealing with and convert where necessary to a common basis.

Coupon Paying Securities

Payment of coupons or dividends during the holding period presents a slight complication unless they occur only at the end. In that case, the yield is simply

$$R = \frac{P_T + C - P_0}{P_0} \tag{1.6}$$

where C represents the coupon payment.

When coupons are paid before the end of the period a problem arises because of the time value of money. Receiving cash flows early should increase the effective yield. There are three ways this can be dealt with fairly easily. First, the problem can be ignored and equation (1.6) used with C equal to the sum of the cash flows occurring during the holding period. This then leaves out of the yield calculation the interest that would be earned by reinvesting intermediate cash flows up to the end of the holding period. Although this procedure obviously introduces an inaccuracy into the calculation, it is the simplest approach and the error may not be large over a short holding period, or if the time between the coupon payment and the end of the period is short.

A second procedure is to assume that all intermediate cash flows are reinvested at the risk-free interest rate up until the end of the holding period.

$$R = \frac{C_{t1} e^{r(T-t1)} + C_{t2} e^{r(T-t2)} + \cdots + P_T - P_0}{P_0}, \tag{1.7}$$

where $t1, t2, \ldots$ represent the dates at which cash flows are received, $C_{t1}, C_{t2}, \ldots$ are the intermediate cash flows, and r is the overnight riskless interest rate, so that the cumulative value of C_{t1} reinvested daily from $t1$ to T would return $C_{t1} e^{r(T-t1)}$ at date T. This brings all of the intermediate payments to the end of the holding period.

The third possibility is to compute the yield as an internal rate of return. R is the yield that makes the present discounted value of all of the cash flows up to the end of the holding period equal to the initial price. That is, R is the rate that makes the following equation hold.

$$P_0 = \frac{C_{t1}}{(1+R)^{t1}} + \frac{C_{t2}}{(1+R)^{t2}} + \cdots + \frac{P_T}{(1+R)^T}. \tag{1.8}$$

The R that is calculated from this expression is the rate per time period, where the unit of time is the same as applies to $t1$ and T. If $t1$ is expressed in years, than R is an annual rate, while if it is in semi-annual periods, it will have to be annualized. The difference between (1.7) and (1.8) is the implicit assumption about the rate at which the intermediate cash flows will be reinvested: Equation (1.7) assumes they are reinvested at the riskless rate, while (1.8) treats them as if they can be reinvested at the internal rate of return.

One place where this problem of how to treat intermediate cash flows occurs is in the computation of the yield to maturity on a bond. Coupon interest for most bonds is paid semiannually in equal installments. A 10 percent coupon bond, for example, will pay its coupon of 5 every six months, starting six months after the date of issue. This means that half of each year's interest is effectively paid six months early. If this were properly taken into account, the yield to maturity on the bond when it was selling at par would be greater than 10 percent. However, by convention, yield to maturity is normally computed by calculating the yield per six-month period (which would be 5 percent in this case) and doubling it to get an annualized figure. Once again, compounding is being used for periods greater than one year and simple interest applied for a shorter period.

Calculating the yield to maturity is a complicated process, which must be done by trial and error. A trial value for R is chosen and the present value of the future cash flows is computed. If this turns out to be above the bond's market price, the R is too low. Higher values are tried until one is found that makes the discounted cash flows sum to less than the price. The yield to maturity is now bracketed and further trial R's are picked, always raising the value when the present value is higher than the price and lowering it when the present value is too small, until the rate is pinned down to the desired degree of accuracy.

Since doing this calculation is time-consuming, various approximations, of varying degrees of accuracy, are in use. Moreover, different conventions exist for treating fractional periods when the yield to maturity of a bond in the middle of a coupon period must be found. The result is that for a given bond, there may be a number of slightly differing published values for its yield to maturity. In this book, we often need to refer to a yield to maturity for a particular bond, and since our data comes from a number of sources, it is quite possible that the reader trying to duplicate our work will find what appear to be small discrepancies. While that situation is unfortunate, it represents a pervasive state of affairs that is not confined to this book.

The following is the formula used by the Treasury to compute the yield to maturity for a bond that has just paid a coupon or is between coupon payments. This covers all of the applications that we will be examining below. R is the yield that makes equation (1.9) hold.

$$(P+A) = \frac{1}{(1+sR/2)}[C/2 + (C/2)a_n + 100v^n], \qquad (1.9)$$

where P is the bond's price,

A is the accrued interest as of the settlement date,

C is the annual coupon,

s is the fraction of a coupon period left before the next payment date ($s = 1$ for a bond that has just paid its coupon),

n is the number of payment periods that will remain *after* the next coupon is paid,

$v^n = (1+R/2)^{-n}$ is the n (semiannual) period discount factor, and

$a_n = (1-v^n)/(R/2)$ is the n period annuity factor.

RISK

The second dimension of interest to an investor is risk. There are different types of risk, including credit risk, the risk of underperformance, unpredictability of returns, and so on. The risk that futures contracts are useful in managing is variability of returns. This is typically measured by the variance of returns or its square root, standard deviation.

The variance is the expected value of the square of the difference between a particular outcome and its mean.

$$\sigma^2 = \text{Var}[R] = E[(R-\bar{R})^2], \qquad (1.10)$$

where σ^2 and $\text{Var}[R]$ denote the variance of the uncertain return R, $\bar{R}$ is the mean of R, and $E[\cdot]$ also denotes the mean or expected value of the expression in brackets. The standard deviation, which we will write as σ (sigma), is generally easier to interpret than the variance because it is in the same units as the mean. For example, for a typical stock the mean annual return might be 15 percent with a standard deviation of 25 percent.

Standard Deviation as the Measure of Risk (A)

Using standard deviation as a measure of risk might be counterintuitive to many investors because return variability on the positive (high) side contributes as much as return variability on the negative (low) side. An investment that returned 40 percent when the expected return was only 12 percent might have a high standard deviation but no one who owned it would be troubled. In our discussion we will use the standard deviation as the appropriate measure of risk for the following reasons: (1) If the returns are approximately normally distributed, the standard deviation (along with the expected return) conveniently summarizes all that we need to know about the distribution of returns; and (2) given the standard deviation, we can easily compute other measures of risk (involving probability of loss or underperformance) that might be more intuitive to the institutional investor.

For instance, assuming returns are normally distributed, if we have estimates of the mean return and the standard deviation, we can easily compute the probability that the return in a given year will be less than some specified level, say x percent. This probability can be written as $N[(x - \bar{R})/\sigma]$, where the value of $N[\bullet]$ evaluated at $(x - \bar{R})/\sigma$ will yield the required probability. $N[\bullet]$ is the cumulative normal distribution function that has been computed and tabulated in the appropriate mathematical tables found in any statistics book.

Example: Suppose $\bar{R}$ is 15 percent and σ is 20 percent. Let us compute the probability of a net loss (i.e., the probability that the return will be less than $x = 0\%$). Given $(x - R)/\sigma = -15\%/20\% = -0.75$, we simply look up the value of $N(-0.75)$. This is found to be equal to 0.227 or 22.7 percent.

For the same return distribution ($R = 15\%$, $\sigma = 20\%$), we can ask a different question: What is the return we can expect with 90 percent confidence? Computing that rate of return, say z, such that there is only 10 percent chance of doing worse is straightforward. The required return z solves the equation:

$$N[(z - \bar{R})/\sigma] = 0.10.$$

From the tables, $0.10 = N[-1.28]$, which implies:

$$(z - 15\%)/20\% = -1.28$$

$$z = -10.6\%.$$

The return on this security has a 10 percent probability of being below -10.6%.

This discussion demonstrates that while other ways of characterizing the notion of risk can certainly be used, in general increased risk by any other measure is also associated with a higher standard deviation. Moreover, standard deviation is relatively easy to calculate and to manipulate mathematically, so we will use it throughout as our risk measure.

ESTIMATING THE EXPECTED YIELD

The reason one is interested in hedging is that interest rates fluctuate and holding period yields are uncertain. Assets with longer maturity than the length of the holding period will have to be sold in the market at a price that is not known. An investment in short-term securities, on the other hand, must be rolled over when they mature, at a reinvestment rate that cannot be predicted with certainty. Even if a security's maturity should coincide with the end of the investor's holding period, yield is uncertain if coupons or dividends are paid within the period and have to be reinvested at rates that are not known today.

The yield concept that we must therefore work with is the expected value of the return. In a statistical sense, expected value corresponds to the idea of an average or mean that would be observed if an experiment were run many times and each outcome recorded. But it is obviously impossible to rerun, say, August 1984 many times to see what the mean return on the stock market really was. Determining expected return over a future holding period is even more difficult since we do not even have one observation to look at. The best one can hope for is to try to uncover empirical regularities in returns from the past that can be expected to continue to hold in the future. One then uses judgment to adjust for the unique features of the current situation.

It should be evident from this discussion that the expected value of an investment's holding period yield is inherently *subjective,* even though theoretical discussions frequently ignore this point. Since judgment plays a central role in forecasting yields, there is no unambiguous best approach. However, a good deal of useful information can be obtained from two types of sources: historical data and current market prices. For both cases, extraction of useful data requires a good theoretical understanding of how a financial market ought to operate.

Estimating Expected Yields from Past Data

Estimating future yields from past data is much harder to do than one would like. Suppose, for example, one wanted to forecast the rate of return of a stock XYZ over the next year. One possible approach would be to take the mean annual return on XYZ over some number of years in the past and assume it would continue to be the same in the future. The first problem with this is in deciding how many past years to include. On the one hand, it is a statistical property of estimating the mean of a series of price changes that if the true mean is constant over time, the accuracy of the estimate depends only on the length of the period considered. Accuracy goes up proportionately with the length of the sample, so that an estimate from ten years of data will be twice as accurate (in terms of variance) as one from five years of data, providing the mean is constant over this period. This is independent of the number of observations within the period that one may have available.

For example, suppose the true mean annual price increase on XYZ is 10 percent and the annual standard deviation is 25 percent, which is representative of a medium to low risk stock. The best estimate of the mean from T years of data is

$$\text{Mean} = \frac{1}{T} \sum_{t=1}^{T} (P_t - P_{t-1}). \tag{1.11}$$

But if all of the terms in the summation were written out, all of the middle ones would cancel, leaving

$$M = \frac{P_T - P_0}{T}. \tag{1.12}$$

The variance of the mean of T independent observations is V^2/T where V^2 is the variance of each observation. In the case of XYZ, the standard deviation of the estimate of the mean from ten years of data is

$$\sqrt{\frac{V^2}{T}} = \frac{V}{\sqrt{T}} = \frac{25}{\sqrt{10}} = 7.90\%.$$

Since the probability that the result of any given trial will be more than 1.0 standard deviation away from the mean is about one-third, there is more than a 30 percent chance that even with ten years of data the observed average return will be more than 8 percent away from the true mean.

From these numbers it is apparent that a large number of past years' data would be required to get very accurate estimates. But this gives rise to the other problem: that all economic phenomena are constantly changing. It is unreasonable to expect mean returns or much of anything else to remain constant for long periods of time. If one extends a data sample far into the past to bring in a longer time period, one incorporates data of less and less relevance to the present. It is clear, for example, that averaging bond yields over periods of high and low inflation is mixing apples and oranges. No improvement in forecast accuracy for the current period can be expected from a sample extended in that way. The result is that there simply may not exist enough data to calculate accurate estimates using equation (1.12).

The way to get the most reliable information out of past data is to focus on things that might be expected to be relatively constant over time. For example, while the level of interest goes up and down with inflation over a fairly wide range, yield *differentials* between different types of securities may be more stable. If one wanted to predict the yield over the next 6 months on a five-year corporate bond, one could use past data to estimate the yield difference between Treasury bills and five-year corporate debt of the same rating and then add this estimated risk premium to today's T-bill rate. This would probably be better than taking the past mean return on five-year bonds directly. Similarly, estimating the expected return on XYZ stock might be done more accurately by taking historical data on the amount by which average returns in the stock market have exceeded risk-free securities (about 8.5 percent according to Ibbotson and Sinquefield[1]) and then applying the Capital Asset Pricing Model, as described in Chapter 6 below, than by looking at XYZ's actual recent performance.

Market Efficiency

An important assumption involved in the kind of estimation procedures we have just discussed is that the prices in financial markets are fairly "efficient" in the sense that they accurately embody the information available to the market. If this were not true, there would be

1. Roger Ibbotson and Rex Sinquefield, *Stocks, Bonds, Bills, and Inflation: 1926–1982* (Charlottesville, Va.: Financial Analysts Research Foundation, 1983).

no reason to expect a security to be priced in the market today so as to pay a yield differential similar to what other securities like it have paid in the past. Fortunately, there is a great deal of evidence that our financial markets are quite efficient. This means that today's market prices themselves convey information about the market's expectations, which can be extracted and used in forecasting. We have just given an example using the current riskless interest rate and an estimate derived from past data of the risk premium the market expects to earn on a particular instrument, to forecast its holding period yield. This calculation depends on the assumption that securities are priced efficiently so that their true expected returns, both now and in the past, include an appropriate risk premium.

There is, however, a danger in assuming too simplistic a relation between market prices and expectations. We will give two examples.

It is tempting to take the yield to maturity on a long-term bond as an estimate of its return in the near future. But while the yield to maturity is the holding period yield over the bond's entire life, it need not be, and normally will not be, its yield over a shorter period. For instance, when the yield curve is "inverted," short-term instruments are trading at higher yields than longer term instruments.

For concreteness, suppose three-month Treasury bills are at 12 percent while twenty-year bonds are at 10 percent. Some people seeing these yields might conclude that T-bills were a better buy since they have lower risk and higher returns, but they would be wrong. An efficient bond market would never really price riskier long-term bonds at a lower expected yield than T-bills. Rather, long-term bonds will be priced so that their expected return over any holding period is enough greater than the riskless rate to compensate risk takers for the extra risk. The 10 percent yield to maturity on long bonds embodies the market's belief that short rates will come down over the life of the bond. The expected yield in the immediate future will be a few percent higher than T-bills, something like 14 percent.

This is not to say that it might not happen in a particular instance that T-bills would outperform long-term debt. Quite the opposite. If long-term debt did not sometimes return less than Treasury bills, it would not really be riskier. But it is important to recognize that if one does forecast a lower yield for twenty-year bonds on occasion, the weight of market opinion is that the return will be considerably higher.

Another case where market prices are sometimes incorrectly taken to be forecasts is in futures. Since a futures price represents a price that one can contract today to trade at in the future, it has been widely argued that the futures price will be bid to the level that best represents the market's expectation of what the price will be on expiration date. This is in general false. As we discuss in detail in Chapter 3, the futures price, for financial instruments in particular, is determined by an arbitrage relation that does not directly involve the expected future spot price at all.

ESTIMATING THE STANDARD DEVIATION

One estimates the standard deviation from a sample of data by estimating the variance and taking the square root. To do this, an estimate of the mean is also needed. When the mean is also estimated from the data sample, the best estimate of the variance is given by

$$\sigma^2 = \frac{1}{T-1} \sum_{t=1}^{T} (R_t - \bar{R})^2, \qquad (1.13)$$

where T is the number of observations in the sample.

The mean $\bar{R}$ is subtracted from each observation, and the results are squared. The sum of squared differences is then divided by the number of observations minus one. (The information in one observation is in a sense used up in estimating the mean.)

The statistical problem we encountered in estimating mean returns — that accuracy required a long time span of data — does not hold when we estimate variance. Theoretically, one can get arbitrarily good variance estimates from a time period of any length by taking observations at shorter and shorter intervals. Accuracy should, therefore, increase as one goes from monthly to weekly to daily data. This reduces the problem of instability over time, since it is not necessary to use data from the distant past. Practically, though, this potential improvement has limits. As one takes shorter and shorter time periods, things like bid-ask spreads and noncontinuous trading that make real world market prices different from the ideal processes of theory begin to play a role. Our feeling is that estimation with weekly or monthly data is perhaps safer than any shorter interval.

MEAN AND VARIANCE IN A PORTFOLIO CONTEXT

A futures hedge always involves putting together futures contracts with a cash market position, such as a portfolio of bonds, in order to produce a combined position with desirable risk and return. We therefore need to know what happens to expected yield and standard deviation when different risky assets are held together.

Combining expected values is straightforward: The expected value of a sum is the sum of the expected values, or

$$E[X+Y] = E[X] + E[Y]. \tag{1.14}$$

For example, X and Y might be the prices per share for two different stocks one year from now. The expected cost of buying one share of each at that time is just the expected price of the first plus the expected price of the second. It is also the case that the expected value of a constant times a random variable is equal to the constant times the expected value — that is,

$$E[CX] = CE[X]. \tag{1.15}$$

It is natural that the expected cost of one hundred shares is one hundred times the expected cost of one share.

In calculating the expected rate of return on a portfolio, one has also to keep track of the fraction each asset makes up of the total portfolio value. For a portfolio containing N securities, the expected return is given by

$$\bar{R}_p = \sum_{n=1}^{N} W_n \bar{R}_n, \tag{1.16}$$

where $\bar{R}_n$ is the expected rate of return on security n, $\bar{R}_p$ is the portfolio expected return, and W_n is the fraction of the initial market value of the portfolio that is held in security n. These portfolio weights will sum to 1.0. In the case where a security is held short, W_n will be negative.

Example: If \$3,000 is invested in a security with an expected return of 10 percent and \$7,000 in one with an expected return of 20 percent, the expected return on the portfolio is

$$\bar{R}_p = (3,000/10,000)(0.10) + (7,000/10,000)(0.20)$$

$$= 17\%.$$

Computing the standard deviation of a sum of random variables is not so easy. The variance of a sum depends on the variances of the individual components, but also on how they move together, their covariance. Covariance is the expected value of the product of the first variable's deviation from its mean times the second variable's deviation from its mean.

$$\text{cov}[X, Y] = \sigma_{XY} = E[(X - \bar{X})(Y - \bar{Y})]. \quad (1.17)$$

If X and Y both go up and down at the same time, covariance will be positive, while if they have no relation to one another, covariance is zero and X and Y are said to be independent. If X is high when Y is low, they will have negative covariance.

Covariance is estimated from a sample of T past observations on X and Y as follows:

$$\text{cov}[X, Y] = \left(\frac{1}{T-1}\right) \sum_{t=1}^{T} (X_t - \bar{X})(Y_t - \bar{Y}). \quad (1.18)$$

The similarity to equation (1.13) for estimating variance is apparent.

Like variance, covariance is sometimes difficult to interpret. For this reason the correlation coefficient is often used. The correlation coefficient ρ (rho) is defined as

$$\rho_{XY} = \frac{\text{cov}[X, Y]}{\sigma_X \sigma_Y}. \quad (1.19)$$

The correlation coefficient is equal to the covariance divided by the product of the two standard deviations.

The correlation coefficient always lies between -1.0 and $+1.0$. Independent variables will have correlation of zero. If Y is always the same number of standard deviations above or below its mean as X is, they are perfectly positively correlated and $\rho = 1.0$, while if they always move in opposite directions $\rho = -1.0$. An effective futures hedge will be one in which the return on the futures position taken has a high negative correlation with that on the item that is being hedged so that their price variations offset each other.

The variance of X plus Y is given by

$$\text{var}[X + Y] = \text{var}[X] + \text{var}[Y] + 2\,\text{cov}[X, Y]. \quad (1.20)$$

And when there are more than two terms in the sum, there will be a covariance term for each separate pair. Thus

$$\text{var}[X + Y + Z] = \text{var}[X] + \text{var}[Y] + \text{var}[Z] + 2\,\text{cov}[X, Y]$$
$$+ 2\,\text{cov}[X, Z] + 2\,\text{cov}[Y, Z]. \quad (1.21)$$

Once again, in calculating the variance of a portfolio's rate of return, it is important to keep track of the portfolio weights on the individual securities. For a two-security portfolio with portfolio weights W_1 and W_2,

$$\text{var}[R_p] = W_1^2 \, \text{var}[R_1] + W_2^2 \, \text{var}[R_2] + 2W_1 W_2 \, \text{cov}[R_1, R_2]. \qquad (1.22)$$

This becomes quite messy for an N-security portfolio:

$$\text{var}(R_p) = \sum_{n=1}^{N} W_n^2 \, \text{var}(R_n) + 2 \sum_{n=2}^{N} \sum_{m=1}^{n-1} W_n W_m \, \text{cov}(R_n, R_m). \qquad (1.23)$$

Equation (1.23) has two sets of terms on the right-hand side. The first represents the N individual variances, each multiplied by the square of its portfolio weight. The second set of terms represents the $(N^2 - N)/2$ covariance terms.

It is apparent that estimating all of the variances and covariances needed to use equation (1.23) on a portfolio with more than a few securities would be painful. Fortunately, we will be able to avoid that in our subsequent calculations by treating portfolios as single securities wherever possible. An example of this is in estimating the mean and standard deviation of returns on a stock portfolio from past data. It is about the same amount of computation to estimate the mean return on each individual stock from its history of returns and then use equation (1.16) to combine them into a portfolio mean as it is to compute the returns on the portfolio for each month in the sample and then take the mean. But in estimating standard deviation it is much simpler just to find the variance of this series of portfolio returns than to compute and combine the variances and covariances for the individual stocks.

SAMPLE COMPUTATION

To illustrate the computations we have described in this chapter, let us take a short series of prices for two stocks, A and B.

Prices: P_A 50   51   54   52   55   57

P_B 20   19   23   23   25   26

Returns: R_A $\dfrac{51-50}{50}$ $\dfrac{54-51}{51}$ $\dfrac{52-54}{54}$ $\dfrac{55-52}{52}$ $\dfrac{57-55}{55}$

R_B $\dfrac{19-20}{20}$ $\dfrac{23-19}{19}$ $\dfrac{23-23}{23}$ $\dfrac{25-23}{23}$ $\dfrac{26-25}{25}$

Returns in percent: R_A 2.0   5.9   −3.7   5.8   3.6

R_B −5.0   21.1   0   8.7   4.0

Mean returns:
$$\bar{R}_A = 1/5(2.0 + 5.9 - 3.7 + 5.8 + 3.6) = 2.72\%$$
$$\bar{R}_B = 1/5(-5.0 + 21.1 + 0 + 8.7 + 4.0) = 5.76\%$$

Variance of returns:
$$\sigma_A^2 = 1/4[(2.0 - 2.72)^2 + (5.9 - 2.72)^2 + (-3.7 - 2.72)^2$$
$$+ (5.8 - 2.72)^2 + (3.6 - 2.72)^2]$$
$$= 15.53.$$

$$\sigma_B^2 = 1/4[(-5.0 - 5.76)^2 + (21.1 - 5.76)^2 + (0 - 5.76)^2$$
$$+ (8.7 - 5.76)^2 + (4.0 - 5.76)^2]$$
$$= 99.00.$$

Standard deviation:
$$\sigma_A = \sqrt{15.53} = 3.94\%$$
$$\sigma_B = \sqrt{99.00} = 9.95\%.$$

Covariance:
$$\sigma_{AB} = 1/4[(2.0 - 2.72)(-5.0 - 5.76)$$
$$+ (5.9 - 2.72)(21.1 - 5.76)$$
$$+ (-3.7 - 2.72)(0 - 5.76)$$
$$+ (5.8 - 2.72)(8.7 - 5.76)$$
$$+ (3.6 - 2.72)(4.0 - 5.76)]$$
$$= 25.25.$$

Correlation:
$$\rho_{AB} = \frac{\sigma_{AB}}{\sigma_A \sigma_B} = \frac{25.25}{(3.94)(9.95)} = 0.64.$$

Now let us use these figures to compute the mean return and standard deviation on a portfolio of three shares of A and five shares of B.

Value of position:
$$A \quad 3 \times 50 = \$150$$
$$B \quad 5 \times 20 = \$100$$
$$\text{Total} = \$250$$

Portfolio weights:
$$W_A = 150/250 = 0.60$$
$$W_B = 100/250 = 0.40$$

Portfolio mean:
$$\bar{R}_p = 0.60\bar{R}_A + 0.40\bar{R}_B = 3.94\%$$

Variance:
$$\sigma_p^2 = (0.60)^2(15.53) + (0.40)^2(99.00)$$
$$+ 2(0.60)(0.40)(25.25)$$
$$= 33.55.$$

Standard
deviation: $\sigma_p = 5.79\%$.

As mentioned, these portfolio figures could have been derived from the series of portfolio returns given by $(0.60R_A + 0.40R_B)$.

2 HEDGING WITH FUTURES CONTRACTS

This chapter will describe how a financial futures hedge is used as a tool for reducing risk. In the next, we will focus on the pricing of financial futures, which determines the cost of hedging. We begin with a discussion of the risk-return trade-off that is possible in a hedged portfolio. The central question of this chapter is how to determine the hedge that has minimum risk. We present an approach based both on the empirical relationship between the value of the item being hedged and the futures contract, and also on a theoretical analysis of this relationship. Strategies for selecting the appropriate futures instrument are discussed, and we end with an analysis of the causes of unhedgeable risk.

Throughout this chapter and the next we concentrate primarily on hedging fixed-income securities against fluctuations in interest rates. A large fraction of many financial institutions' hedging needs fall in this area. The futures contracts most useful for this are those based on Treasury bills, ten-year Treasury notes, and twenty-year Treasury bonds. However, while the institutional details of other cash instruments and futures markets are different, the hedging principles we present here are widely applicable elsewhere.

DEFINING THE RISK: MICRO AND MACRO HEDGING

The first step for a financial institution contemplating an interest rate hedging program is to decide precisely what the objective of the hedge is: What is the precise exposure that is being hedged? There are two basic approaches, often known as "micro" and "macro" hedging. In micro hedging, each asset or liability to be hedged is taken separately. For example, if a firm is holding a portfolio of government bonds and also has written a guaranteed interest contract, micro hedging might lead to one hedge in which Treasury bond futures were sold short against the bonds and a second in which bond futures were purchased to hedge the GIC commitment. The two hedges would then involve offsetting positions in the bond futures market, obviously a duplication.

The focus of a macro hedging program is to eliminate or reduce the effect of interest rate fluctuations on the hedger's total assets and liabilities or, more generally, on his income statement and balance sheet. To do this effectively, it is important to identify correctly the *overall* net risk exposure. This involves analyzing assets and liabilities by group, by maturity, and, if relevant, by division or profit center within the institution. When assets and liabilities match with respect to size, credit type, maturity, and general quality, they provide each other natural hedges. Only to the extent that they are mismatched will there be interest rate exposure.

Financial institutions typically have a multitude of interest-rate-sensitive assets and liabilities on the balance sheet, so that identifying the precise nature of the asset/liability mismatch and the resulting interest rate risk may be very difficult. While micro hedging does forego the savings of effort and transactions costs that macro hedging makes possible, its relative ease of implementation makes it the preferred approach for an institution just starting a hedging program.

RISK-RETURN POSSIBILITIES

In designing a hedge program, it is not always optimal to eliminate all risk by hedging (when this is possible) or even to minimize the risk of the hedge portfolio. There is a cost to hedging: Reducing risk also lowers expected returns. The degree of risk exposure that should be retained in a hedged position is therefore an important decision. It will depend on several factors including management's risk tolerance, its expectations about the movement of the underlying prices, and the amount of capital employed. One of the great values of futures contracts is that they allow management to *choose* the level of risk that will be borne on a given investment.

Let us consider the following example as an illustration of how the risk and return of a hedged portfolio change as the number of futures contracts traded increases. Suppose that an insurance company wishes to hedge its net interest exposure over the next six months on a position in government bonds currently selling at par of 100. This is done by selling Treasury bond futures contracts.

Let the current value of the bond position be $1 million and assume the expected value and standard deviation of its value in six months are estimated to be $1.1 million and $40 thousand, respectively. The various risk-return possibilities for hedged positions involving different numbers of futures contracts might be as shown below.

Number of futures contracts	Expected profit ($ thousand)	Standard deviation of profit
0	100	40.0
1	95	35.6
2	90	31.3
3	85	27.3
4	80	23.7
5	75	20.6
6	70	18.4
7	65	17.5
8	60	17.9
10	50	19.6
20	0	22.4

It is clear that the hedge that produces maximum risk reduction is to sell somewhere around seven contracts. After that the risk of the portfolio position increases.

In general, selling futures contracts against a security position reduces expected return and risk, up to a point of minimum risk. The combinations of risk and expected return that can be achieved lie along a curve like the one shown in Figure 2–1. The exact location of this curve — how much return must be given up to achieve a particular risk level; how much risk is left after all that can be hedged has been eliminated; and, in particular, how many futures contracts must be sold to achieve the risk minimizing position — depends on a number of factors, each of which we will discuss in detail below. However, the risk-return trade-off in a hedged position will always have the general shape shown in Figure 2–1.

Figure 2–1. Risk–Return Trade-off in Short Hedge.

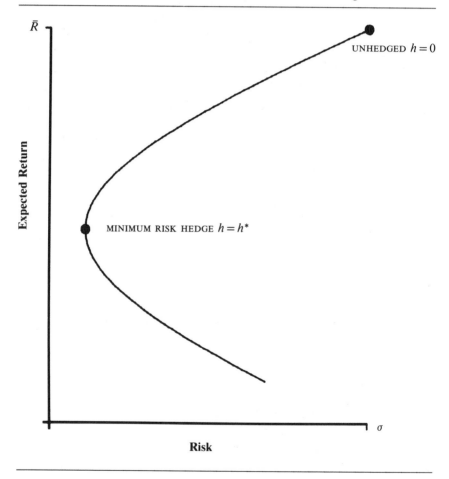

It is easiest to analyze a hedge in terms of its "hedge ratio," for which we will use the symbol h. The hedge ratio represents the number of units of futures traded per unit of the cash securities held. The most convenient way to define units varies from security to security. For example, a Treasury bond futures contract is based on $100,000 face value of bonds and prices are quoted on the basis of par $= 100$. This means that one bond contract can be thought of as representing 1,000 "units" of futures. For stock index futures, a different definition is more useful, as we will describe in Chapter 6.

If $h = 0$, the return and risk are just those for the unhedged position. As h is increased, one moves down the risk-return possibility curve, until the risk-minimizing position is reached. We will denote the hedge ratio for the minimum risk hedge as h^*. Beyond h^*, the risk begins to increase, as the risk taken on by trading futures contracts begins to outweigh the risk that has been hedged away. One of the major goals of this chapter is to show how estimates of h^* may be computed, either by statistical methods using past observations on price movements for the item being hedged or by analytical treatment of its characteristics such as maturity, coupon rate, and bond rating. But first we will develop the expressions for expected return and standard deviation in a hedged position as a function of the hedge ratio.

The Expected Return and Standard Deviation in a Hedged Position

Let P_0 be the initial price of one unit of the cash position (e.g., 100 in the case of a bond selling at par). Denote the price of the cash securities at the end of the holding period as $\tilde{P}_1$ where the symbol ~ indicates that this price is a random or uncertain variable as of the beginning of the holding period. Let $\bar{P}_1$ be the mean of $\tilde{P}_1$, and σ_p be the standard deviation of $\tilde{P}_1 - P_0$.

The symbols F_0 and $\tilde{F}_1$ will refer to the initial and ending futures prices, with $\bar{F}_1$ denoting the mean of $\tilde{F}_1$ and σ_f denoting the standard deviation of the futures price change.

The hedge will consist of a short position in h units of futures per unit of the cash position. Finally, assume that the correlation between the price of the cash portfolio and the futures price is ρ.

The profit per unit on the hedged portfolio is the price change on the cash position minus h times the change in the futures price.

$$\text{Profit} = (\tilde{P}_1 - P_0) - h(\tilde{F}_1 - F_0). \tag{2.1}$$

The expected profit is then

$$\text{Expected Profit} = (\bar{P}_1 - P_0) - h(\bar{F}_1 - F_0). \tag{2.2}$$

The variance and standard deviation of the profit, σ_h, are given by equations (2.3) and (2.4):

$$\sigma_h^2 = \sigma_p^2 + h^2\sigma_f^2 - 2\rho h\sigma_p\sigma_f \tag{2.3}$$

$$\sigma_h = \sqrt{\sigma_p^2 + h^2\sigma_f^2 - 2\rho h\sigma_p\sigma_f}. \tag{2.4}$$

To generate the combinations of risk and expected return that are feasible in a given hedge as shown in Figure 2-1, it is only necessary to plug different values of h into equations (2.2) and (2.4). The risk minimizing h^* can be derived using calculus by setting the derivative of σ_h^2 with respect to h equal to zero in equation (2.3). The result of the derivation is that h^* is the covariance between the price change of the cash position and the price change of the futures contract, divided by the variance of the price change of the futures contract, or

$$h^* = \frac{\text{cov}(P_1 - P_0, F_1 - F_0)}{\text{var}(F_1 - F_0)}, \tag{2.5}$$

which can also be expressed as:

$$h^* = \frac{\rho\sigma_p}{\sigma_f}. \tag{2.6}$$

As we will discuss in more detail below, an estimate of h^* is easily computed in practice by running a regression of cash price changes on futures price changes. The slope of the regression line is h^*.

Substituting equation (2.6) into equation (2.4) yields the minimum risk that can be attained on a hedge portfolio using the chosen futures contracts:

$$\sigma_h(\text{min}) = \sigma_p\sqrt{1 - \rho^2}. \tag{2.7}$$

From equation (2.7) we observe another important aspect of the risk-return possibilities of hedged portfolios: For a given futures contract with correlation coefficient ρ, the risk cannot be completely eliminated even using a risk-minimizing hedge. This is only possible when there is perfect correlation, with $\rho = 1$ or $\rho = -1$. Otherwise there will always be some unhedgeable residual risk. How much of this risk there is will depend on how close ρ is to 1 or -1. In general, the best futures contract for a hedge is the one with highest correlation with the cash position.

COMPUTING THE NUMBER OF FUTURES CONTRACTS NEEDED

We will now describe how the number of futures contracts needed to produce the minimum risk hedge can be estimated. The most direct approach to this question involves estimating h^* from a regression analysis of the past price changes on the item being hedged and the futures contract to be used. However, in many cases this kind of regression is not feasible, because past prices are unavailable. We then describe alternative methods that derive an estimate of h^* as the product of a series of factors, each adjusting for a specific characteristic of the item being hedged (coupon and maturity), or of the futures contract (basis risk, and the effect of marking to market).

Estimating h^* by Linear Regression

A very useful statistical technique in hedging analysis is linear regression. Regression analysis fits a relationship between a dependent or y variable and a set of explanatory or x variables, when historical data series corresponding to each are available. The resulting linear equation is the one that produces the smallest errors between the actual values of the dependent variable and those estimated by the equation.

In a two-variable regression of the form

$$y = a + bx + \epsilon, \tag{2.8}$$

a represents the intercept on the y-axis and b represents the slope of the regression line. ϵ (epsilon) denotes the regression residual, the part of y that is not related to x. By the mathematics of regression, the coefficient b is equal to the covariance between y and x divided by the variance of x in the data sample that the regression is run on.

When data are available on the past price changes of the item being hedged (DP) and the futures contract that will be used in the hedge (DF), then running the regression

$$DP = a + bDF \qquad\qquad (2.9)$$

yields

$$b = \frac{\text{cov}(DP, DF)}{\text{var}(DF)}.$$

The regression coefficient b is the hedge ratio (the number of units of futures per unit of the cash position) that would have minimized the standard deviation of the value of a hedged position over the time period covered by the regression data.

For example, the following are the monthly price changes during 1983 for the U.S. Treasury 11¾s of 2001 bonds (DP) and for the nearest to expiration Treasury bond futures contract (DF).

DP	DF
−4.219	−3.313
4.313	3.969
−1.781	−0.719
2.968	2.969
−4.562	−4.281
−0.844	0.313
−4.906	−4.438
−1.406	−0.156
3.687	3.500
−1.937	−2.031
1.063	0.938
−1.313	−1.031

Regressing DP on DF gives

$$DP = -0.359 + 1.08 DF \qquad\qquad R^2 = 0.97$$

$$\text{Standard error of regression} = 0.55.$$

The minimum risk hedge ratio for these bonds during 1983 was, therefore, 1.08.

We have also given two summary statistics for the regression, R^2, and the standard error of regression. R^2 is a measure of the success of a least squares fit. It measures the fraction of the variance of the dependent or y-variable that can be explained by its relation to the independent or x-variable. R^2 has a value between zero and unity, with a higher R^2 denoting a better fit of the regression line.

In the application of regression analysis to a futures hedge, R^2 is a widely used measure of hedging effectiveness since it gives the fraction of the cash position's variance that is eliminated by the hedge. R^2 can be expressed mathematically in several ways, including the following:

$$R^2 = \rho^2$$
$$= \frac{(\text{cov}[DP, DF])^2}{(\text{var}[DP])(\text{var}[DF])} \qquad (2.10)$$

where ρ is the correlation coefficient between DP and DF.

A related statistic often produced by regression programs, and of considerable interest to a hedger, is the standard error of regression. This is the standard deviation of the regression residuals, or differences between the actual DP and the regression line. In the case of a futures hedge, these differences are the random price changes in the cash position that were not offset by the futures. The standard error of regression is, therefore, the minimum risk of a hedged position, as given above in equation (2.7). The output of standard regression packages systematically give the above information as well as other related statistical measures.

Estimating h^* from Bond Characteristics

Unfortunately, it is not always possible to run a regression to estimate the risk-minimizing hedge ratio. The security to be hedged may be a new issue or a private placement that does not have a past trading history to work with. And even when sufficient past data are available, one might still not wish to rely too heavily on regression results for a bond with only a short term left to maturity because its risk properties change over time as maturity approaches and its behavior in the past may no longer be representative of what one may expect in the future.

In any case, it is possible to derive an estimate of h^* from first principles, as the product of a series of adjustment factors. These factors allow us to approximate the probable relationship between DP and DF, based on the characteristics of the item being hedged and the futures contract. That is, we will adjust explicitly for the factors that regression takes into account implicitly.

Adjusting the Hedge to Produce Dollar Equivalence

Yields for similar securities move together to a large extent. Two long-term government bonds, for example, will have yields that are approximately equal, and change together over time. But a given change in yield can result in much different price changes if the bonds differ in coupon or maturity.

To illustrate how the change in the price of a futures contract or a cash instrument caused by a given interest rate change depends on the maturity, coupon, and price of the instrument, Table 2-1 below shows the equivalent value of 1 percent rise in the interest rate from 10 percent to 11 percent for a number of maturity and coupon combinations.

Table 2-1.   The Value of a 1% Change in Yield for Various Cash Securities and Futures Contracts.

Instrument	Price at 10%	Price at 11%	Value of Change
90-day Treasury bill	97.50	97.25	0.25
180-day Treasury bill	95.00	94.50	0.50
1-year Treasury bill	90.00	89.00	1.00
5-year 8% coupon bond	92.28	88.69	3.58
5-year 12% coupon bond	107.72	103.77	3.95
10-year 8% coupon bond	87.54	82.07	5.46
10-year 12% coupon bond	112.46	105.98	6.49
20-year 8% coupon bond	82.84	75.93	6.91
20-year 12% coupon bond	117.16	108.02	9.14
30-year 8% coupon bond	81.07	73.83	7.25
30-year 12% coupon bond	118.93	108.72	10.20
Treasury bill futures contract ($1,000,000 face value)	90.00	89.00	$2,500
Treasury note futures contract ($100,000 face value)	87.54	82.07	$5,463
Treasury bond futures contract ($100,000 face value)	82.84	75.93	$6,910

Since an effective hedge requires that the profit or loss on futures must offset the cash instrument's change in value *in dollars,* an adjustment for differences in coupon and maturity between the underlying bond for the futures contract and the position being hedged must be made, so that an equal yield change on the two instruments results in an equal dollar change in the values of the cash and futures positions. This is known variously as achieving "dollar equivalence," "maturity adjustment," or "weighting the hedge."

The general principle of the adjustment to produce dollar equivalence is that the effect in dollars of a given interest rate change over the hedging period should be the same for the cash instrument and the futures contracts held. This principle applies in all situations where changes in interest rates provide the primary source of changes in value in the cash instrument and the futures instrument. This adjustment can be done in various ways, some more accurate than others.

One procedure that is widely suggested and is easy to implement, but does not give accurate answers in all cases, is to use the conversion factor specified by the delivery terms of the futures contract as a hedge ratio. Although we do not recommend this approach in general, it is useful to describe how it works as an introduction to computing dollar equivalence by more exact means.

Most futures contracts allow delivery of a variety of different instruments. The futures price is quoted based on a specific reference security, such as a twenty-year 8 percent Treasury bond in the case of the Chicago Board of Trade's T-bond contract, but other bonds with different maturities or coupons can be delivered. If they are, the invoice price to be paid will be computed by multiplying the futures price by a conversion factor specific to the bonds being delivered. This adjusts for the fact that $100,000 face value of another bond will not cost the same as $100,000 face value of the reference bond, when they have the same yield. The conversion factor is the price (as a fraction of par of 100) that the bond being delivered would have if it were yielding 8 percent. The result is that if the futures price changes by 1.00, the *effective* futures price change to someone planning to make delivery is equal to 1.00 times the conversion factor on the bond that will be delivered.

Example: Suppose that the cash position to be hedged was $2 million face value of the 14 percent coupon issue of 2011. For September 1982 delivery the conversion or delivery factor published by the CBT for calculating delivery prices of this bond was 1.6359. While twenty futures contracts would have had the same face value as this position, if the bonds were going to be delivered against the futures contracts, proper hedging would have had to take into account the conversion ratio. Given the price factor on the bonds actually held, $20 \times 1.6359 = 33$ contracts were indicated.

The idea behind the use of the conversion factor in setting the hedge ratio here is that a change in bond yields that leads to a change of 1.00 in the value of the twenty-year 8 percent reference bond (when it is selling at par) will result in a price change for the bond being hedged equal to 1.00 times 1.6359. In order for the resulting change in the value of the futures hedge to offset this, 1.6359 dollars worth of futures (in terms of face value) must be sold per dollar of cash bonds.

Unfortunately, using the conversion factor as a hedge ratio will produce dollar equivalence only under limited circumstances. One is when the market bond yield is 8 percent and the reference bond is selling at par. However, this does not continue to hold true for most bonds as market yields move away from 8 percent. When yields change, given the set of conversion factors, one bond will become "cheapest to deliver," meaning that the cost of buying the quantity necessary to make delivery on the futures contract is less for that bond than for any other currently trading. We will discuss this issue further in the next chapter. At market yields away from 8 percent, using the conversion factor as the hedge ratio produces dollar equivalence only for the cheapest to deliver bond. (At 8 percent, all bonds are equally cheap for delivery.)

The hedge ratio needed for dollar equivalence is the price change for the bonds being hedged divided by the futures price change that will result from a given change in market yields. We will approach this problem in two parts, first finding the yield sensitivity of the cash securities relative to the underlying asset for the futures contract and then adjusting for the relative price change between the underlying asset and the futures contract.

The following procedure can be used to compute the relative interest rate sensitivities of the two cash instruments. Let P refer to the price of the securities being hedged and let P_U be the price of the underlying asset for the futures contract. R and R_U are their respective yields to maturity. What we want is the ratio of the price change for the security being hedged caused by a given change in its yield (DP), divided by the price change for the underlying asset of the future (DP_U) caused by the same yield change, DR. In other words,

$$\text{Relative yield sensitivity} = (DP/DR)/(DP_U/DR).$$

These factors can be calculated directly from current prices, yields, coupon rates, and maturities.

Taking the cash market instrument first, compute its yield to maturity, call it R_0. Next, compute the price the bonds would have at a slightly different yield R_1, say ten basis points lower ($DR = -0.10\%$), by taking the present value of the stream of coupons and principal at that yield. Call this price P_1 while the actual price is P_0. Then $DP = (P_1 - P_0)$.

DP_U is computed the same way. The ratio of these two numbers is then the adjustment factor that produces dollar equivalence. Since the yield change in the denominator DR is the same for both, the last equation becomes DP/DP_U.

$$\text{Relative yield sensitivity} = DP/DP_U, \text{ given } DR. \qquad (2.11)$$

Notice that the interest sensitivity of a bond's price will change as the price and time to maturity change, so it is necessary to recompute this ratio periodically, especially after a major change in prices. Assuming the yields move perfectly together — both between the cash security being hedged and the underlying asset of the futures contract, and between the underlying asset and the future — the weighted hedge ratio that will produce dollar equivalence should be the relative yield sensitivity factor given by equation (2.11).

Example: Suppose the price P_0 of a thirty-year 11 percent coupon Treasury bond is currently 94.21. Its yield to maturity R_0 is computed as 11.70 percent. If the yield were to drop by ten basis points to 11.60 (R_1), the bond's price would rise to 95.00 (P_1).

We have

$$DP = 95.00 - 94.21 = 0.785.$$

For the reference 8 percent, twenty-year bond the prices at yields of 11.70 and 11.60 are, respectively, 71.63 and 72.22, so

$$DP_U = 72.22 - 71.63 = 0.590.$$

The relative yield sensitivity is therefore

$$DP/DP_U = 0.785/0.590 = 1.33.$$

An important point that this example has left out is that the true underlying asset for the futures contract is *not* the reference bond;

it is the bond that is cheapest to deliver against the futures contract. Relative yield sensitivity should be calculated between the bonds being hedged and the cheapest to deliver bond (divided by its delivery factor in order to express the result in terms of the futures price).

In recent years, one of the cheapest to deliver bonds has nearly always been the Treasury 7⅝ of 2007, with a delivery factor of 0.9660 as of May 1985. This bond is quite close to the reference bond in terms of coupon and maturity, which suggests that it would not have made a great deal of difference if yield sensitivities were computed with respect to a twenty-year 8 percent bond instead. But this situation need not continue in the future, so one should use the cheapest to deliver bond in this calculation.

We will return to the calculation of relative yield sensitivity again in Chapter 5, where we will examine a more rigorous approach based on the concept of "duration."

"Tailing" the Hedge: Adjustment for Mark to Market Settlement

In our discussion so far, we have ignored the impact of mark to market settlement. The mechanics of futures trading call for each outstanding contract to be marked to market daily at the settlement price for the day. Any paper profit accruing to a position since the previous day's settlement is deposited in the trader's margin account in cash, and any loss is deducted from the margin account to be passed to accounts on the winning side.

Marking to market has an effect on the risk minimizing hedge ratio. As we will show in the next chapter, theoretically an increase of 1.00 in price for the underlying cash security to the futures contract should lead to a futures price rise such that its *present value* is 1.00. This futures price change can be approximated by $(1.00)e^{rT}$ where r is the current riskless interest rate and T is the time to expiration of the futures contract. Because the future is marked to market daily, this price change would generate an immediate cash flow.

Consider a hedge in which futures were sold to hedge a position in the reference bond. If a hedge ratio of 1.0 were used, an increase of 1.00 in the cash price would be *more* than offset by a cash outflow of $(1.00)e^{rT}$ on the futures. To achieve dollar equivalence, it is necessary to reduce the hedge ratio by multiplying it by e^{-rT}, in essence taking the present value of h^*. This adjustment is known as "tailing" the hedge.

Example: Suppose that after adjusting for relative yield sensitivity the best estimate of h^* for a given bond position is 1.20. The hedge is to be put on using a future with six months to expiration, and the current short term riskless rate is 6.00 percent. Compounding continuously over the six-month futures life gives a discount factor of $e^{-(0.06)(6/12)} = 0.970$. The present value of the hedge ratio is therefore $h^* = (1.20)(0.970) = 1.16$, the value that adjusts for the mark to market settlement feature.

As this example shows, tailing the hedge does not make a very big difference when interest rates are low and the time to expiration is not too long. However, some futures contracts have expirations up to three years in the future. If a long-term hedge is contemplated using a distant contract, adjusting the hedge ratio for the mark to market effect can be important.

Adjusting for Basis Risk

Setting the hedge ratio to produce dollar equivalence adjusts for the relative size of price changes that will result from an equal yield change on the item being hedged and the underlying security for the futures contract. But the yields for different bonds do not always change by the same amount. Moreover, the futures price does not move exactly in line with the price of its underlying asset. Less than perfect correlation between changes in the value of the cash position and the futures price is a major factor that must be dealt with in designing a hedge.

Textbook illustrations of futures hedges often show how the hedge eliminates risk for a position in the underlying asset, because the cash market price and the futures price must converge at expiration. In these examples, a one-for-one hedge, $h = 1.0$, fully eliminates risk: The cash position can always be simply delivered in fulfillment of the short futures contracts to lock in the price originally contracted for. Delivery of a different coupon or maturity bond does not affect the performance of the hedge as long as the delivery factor has been properly incorporated into the hedge ratio.

The problem with this illustration is that the circumstances it describes occur very rarely. For one thing, many hedges involve cash securities that are not deliverable against the futures contract. Further, when the cash securities are deliverable, there are still only four expiration dates per year for each futures contract. While the futures market will be tied *fairly* closely to the cash market at all times by arbitrage (as we will describe more fully in the next chapter), except on the precise expiration date there is always some latitude for independent price movement. This means that if a hedge is to be lifted by offsetting the futures position in the futures market rather than by delivery, there will be uncertainty about whether the gain or loss on the hedge will *exactly* offset the change in value of the cash position, even for a hedge of the underlying deliverable securities. The risk of slippage in the relation between the futures price and the price of the underlying asset is called basis risk.

How large this risk is will depend on a number of factors, including how far the futures are from expiration at the time the hedge is lifted (the further from expiration, the larger the potential risk) and how closely tied the cash and futures markets are. Treasury bills have very little basis risk while stock index futures have relatively large basis risk. Treasury bonds fall in between, though closer to bills than to stock indexes in their degree of basis risk. One last cause of basis risk is the possibility that the cheapest to deliver instrument will change over time, altering the way the futures price relates to the cash market.

Hedging with futures is frequently described as exchanging absolute price risk for basis risk. In this case, the term is being used in a broader sense to refer to relative price movements between the cash position being hedged and the futures contract, not just between the future and its underlying security. Throughout this book we will use the expression "basis risk" in this more inclusive sense to mean all residual risk in a hedge that can not be eliminated by trading futures.

Basis risk alters both the effectiveness of a hedge and also the value of the risk-minimizing hedge ratio. Estimating the hedge ratio by regression adjusts implicity for the normal degree of basis risk between the cash securities and the futures contract. Adjusting explicitly for basis risk is more problematical. A general result is that the larger basis risk is, the smaller will be the risk-minimizing hedge ratio. Intuitively, this is because the contribution of basis risk to overall hedge variability increases as the futures position taken becomes larger. Since hedging is trading off absolute price risk for basis risk, the more basis risk is present, the less favorable that trade-off becomes and the smaller should be the futures position that is the source of the basis risk.

It is, therefore, appropriate in most cases to reduce the hedge ratio below the level that is indicated by the calculations we have already described. How much it should be reduced will depend on the amount of basis risk that is expected to be present. At this point, there is no generally accepted method (aside from estimating the hedge ratio by regression) for computing exactly how far the hedge ratio should be lowered. Indeed, the impact of basis risk on the optimal hedge ratio is frequently ignored in discussions of hedging. We will leave this important issue as an open question at this time and return to it again in an advanced section below.

Calculating the Number of Contracts to Achieve the Desired Hedge Ratio

We have discussed two ways to estimate the minimum risk hedge ratio h^*. Now we will calculate the number of futures contracts needed to achieve this hedge ratio.

If P is the price per unit of the cash position and F is the price per unit of the futures contract, h^* gives the number of units of futures per unit of cash securities needed in the hedged position. Multiplying h^* by the total number of cash units held, call this N_C, gives the number of futures units needed. Dividing by the number of futures units in a contract S (for "size") then gives the number of contracts to trade.

$$\text{Number of futures contracts} = \frac{h^* N_C}{S}. \qquad (2.12)$$

This general formula can be made more intuitive in the case of fixed income securities and futures based on them, because all prices are quoted on the basis of par value equal to 100 (i.e., one unit of cash or futures is \$100 face value of the security in question). In that case, the total face value of the cash position is $100 N_C$, and the face value of a futures contract is $100 S$. Equation (2.12) can then be written:

$$\text{Number of futures contracts} = h^* \frac{\text{Face value of cash position}}{\text{Face value of futures contract}}. \qquad (2.13)$$

Example: To achieve a hedge ratio of 1.5 on a bond portfolio containing \$2 million face value of Treasury bonds, $(1.5) \times 20 = 30$ T-bond futures contracts, each of face value \$100,000, should be sold.

Summary of Procedure for Determining the
Risk-Minimizing Hedge

Let us summarize the procedure we have described for estimating the risk-minimizing hedge. The first step is to choose a futures contract that has high correlation with the price movements on the position to be hedged. Normally the contract with the highest correlation coefficient is chosen, except when liquidity is a problem, as we will discuss more fully below.

If past data are available on price changes on the item being hedged and on the future, the regression of DP on DF, as in equation (2.9), will yield a good estimate of the risk minimizing h^*. This will adjust for coupon and maturity effects, marking to market in the futures, and imperfect correlation between the cash market instrument and the futures contract.

When the regression on past price changes cannot be run, an approximate value for h^* can be derived as a product of factors adjusting for these effects separately, as follows:

1. The factor for coupon and maturity effects is computed as described in the section on dollar equivalence. One calculates the changes in present value that are caused by a given small movement in yield to maturity for the coupon and principal payments of the position being hedged and the cheapest to deliver bond for the futures contract. The conversion factor for the cheapest to deliver bond is then used to convert its price sensitivity into the price sensitivity implied for the futures contract. Dividing the cash price sensitivity by the futures price sensitivity yields the first factor.

2. The second factor corrects for the effect of marking to market of the futures contracts, by discounting the hedge ratio based on yield sensitivity alone back to the present. Thus, the second factor is the discount factor e^{-rT}, where r is the short-term riskless interest rate and T is the time to expiration of the futures contract.

3. One should adjust for the basis risk between the cash securities and the futures contract. The product of the first two factors should be reduced, to a greater or lesser extent, depending on the amount of basis risk anticipated in the hedge. This adjustment is essentially a matter of judgment, though some idea of the appropriate order of magnitude can be gained from comparing theoretical hedge ratios to those fitted by regression for similar securities to the ones being hedged.

Once a value for h^* has been arrived at, it is translated into the required number of futures contracts for the hedge by using equation (2.12). The number of contracts is h^* times the size of the position being hedged divided by the size of one futures contract. For all fixed income securities quoted on the basis of par equals 100, the number of futures contracts is just h^* times the face value of the position being hedged divided by the face value of one futures contract.

Since all of these adjustment coefficients may change through time, it is important to recompute the hedge ratio periodically. This is especially relevant when h^* has been estimated from the regression on prices in the case of a security with short maturity. The maturity effect will change as time progresses.

A Complete Example

Suppose a pension fund manager wanted to minimize risk due to interest rate fluctuations on a $10 million face value position in U.S. Treasury 14s of 2011 beginning on 16 November 1984 (immediately after the November coupon was paid). The bonds were currently selling for 114.60, and at that time they had twenty-seven years to maturity, but they are callable in 2006. We will therefore treat them as twenty-two-year instruments. The riskless interest rate was 8.00 percent. The December Treasury bond future had 35 days to expiration.

The factors called for are as follows:

Yield Sensitivity Factor: The yield to maturity at 114.60 is 12.09 percent. The price at a yield of 11.99 percent would be 115.47. Assume that the 7⅝ of February 2007 were the cheapest delivery bonds at that time. Their prices at yields of 12.09 percent and 11.99 percent would be 67.66 and 68.20. The conversion factor was 0.9802. The factor is therefore

$$\frac{(115.47 - 114.60)}{(68.20 - 67.66)} \times 0.9802 = 1.58.$$

$$\text{Discount factor} = e^{-0.08(35/365)} = 0.992.$$

The approximate h^* with no adjustment for basis risk is therefore

$$h^* = (1.58)(0.992) = 1.57.$$

$$\frac{\text{FACE VALUE OF CASH POSITION}}{\text{FACE VALUE OF FUTURES CONTRACT}} = \frac{\$10,000,000}{\$100,000} = 100,$$

which implies that the risk-minimizing hedge is estimated to require $100 \times 1.57 = 157$ T-bond contracts to be sold against the long bond position.

It is worthwhile to compare this estimate of h^* with one computed by regression. The data are the end of month prices for the Treasury 14s and the Chicago Board of Trade bond futures contract, from June 1982 through October 1984.

$$DC = -0.198 \quad + \quad 1.521\,DF \qquad R^2 = 0.977.$$
$$(0.0166) \quad (0.00192)$$

In this case, the two are quite close.

BASIS RISK AND HEDGING EFFECTIVENESS CONTINUED (A)

By the mathematics of regression, regressing price changes for the cash instrument on those of the futures contract produces the hedge ratio that would have minimized the variance in the dollar value of the hedged position. It therefore automatically takes care of the dollar equivalence and tailing adjustments that we discussed in the previous section. When those adjustments were made explicitly, we assumed that the yields for the cash securities and the futures contract moved by exactly the same amount. Unfortunately, they normally do not, which leads to basis risk. In this section, we will examine the magnitude of basis risk a little more closely and offer some empirical results on its consequences for hedging effectiveness.

First we will look at the effect of basis risk on hedges of several long-term Treasury bonds with the Treasury bond futures contract. We will run the regression (2.9) in two different ways: regressing price changes in the cash instrument on price changes in the futures contract, then regressing yield changes in the cash instrument on yield changes in the futures contract. The first regression will give estimates of h^*, which can be compared to those computed explicitly by the alternative method. The second regression will show how closely the yields in different segments of the long-term government bond market move together with those of the futures contract.

The data are end-of-month values from June 1982 through October 1984 for four Treasury bonds and the nearest to expiration CBT bond futures contract. The maturities of the four bonds span the longer end of the government bond market from about nine years to about twenty-nine years. They were selected partly because they had been fairly recently issued and a liquid cash market existed for them. Because of the restrictions on the T-bond contract, the two shorter maturity issues were not deliverable during this period.

For the future, the yield to maturity is calculated assuming the futures price is that of the 8 percent coupon twenty-year reference bond. In each category, DP refers to changes in prices of the cash instrument, DF refers to changes in prices of the T-bond futures contract, DY refers to changes in yields of the cash instrument and DFY refers to changes in yields of the futures contract. Standard errors for the estimates of the coefficients are shown in parentheses. The value for h^* computed by the alternative method is its value as of 31 October 1984, the end of the sample period, under the assumption that the 7⅝ of 2007 bonds would be the cheapest to deliver.

Cash Instrument: U.S. Treasury 13¾s of May 1992

$$DP = -0.055 \quad + \quad 0.962\,DF \qquad R^2 = 0.915$$
$$ (0.026) \qquad (0.003)$$

$$DY = \quad 0.007 \quad + \quad 0.904\,DFY \qquad R^2 = 0.915$$
$$ (0.00087) \quad (0.00269)$$

h^* computed by alternative method: 0.96

Cash Instrument: Treasury 10⅜s of May 1995

$$DP = -0.067 \quad + \quad 1.041\,DF \qquad R^2 = 0.942$$
$$ (0.020) \qquad (0.00236)$$

$$DY = \quad 0.020 \quad + \quad 0.952\,DFY \qquad R^2 = 0.956$$
$$ (0.00048) \quad (0.00148)$$

h^* computed by alternative method: 1.05

Cash Instrument: Treasury 11¾s of February 2001

$$DP = -0.131 \quad + \quad 1.219\,DF \qquad R^2 = 0.969$$
$$ (0.0145) \quad (0.00167)$$

$$DY = \quad 0.0198 \quad + \quad 0.906\,DFY \qquad R^2 = 0.973$$
$$ (0.00026) \quad (0.00081)$$

h^* computed by alternative method: 1.20

Cash Instrument: Treasury 14s of November 2011

$$DP = -0.198 + 1.521\,DF \qquad R^2 = 0.977$$
$$\quad\;\;(0.0166)\quad (0.00192)$$

$$DY = \;\;0.020 + 0.874\,DFY \qquad R^2 = 0.974$$
$$\quad\;\;(0.00023)\quad (0.00072)$$

h^* computed by alternative method: 1.58

These regressions reveal several things. First, there is little difference among them in R^2. The equations based on yield changes fit just as well as those on price changes. Also the high R^2s mean the different bonds seem to be quite "hedgeable," with the longer bonds somewhat more so than the shorter. This shows that yield movements for these bonds are highly correlated with the futures contract, so basis risk is small.

The second thing one sees is that while the regression coefficients in the yield change equations are all quite close together, around 0.9, the price change equations show much different values. h^* for the 13¾ of 1992 is 0.96 while it is more than 50 percent larger, 1.52, for the 14s of 2011. Because a given percent change in yield produces a much larger change in the long bond's price, a bigger futures position is required to hedge it.

As a consequence, as we found in our example of the previous section, there is very little difference between the h^* estimated from the regression and the h^* computed from the characteristics of these bonds. We can conclude from these results that in a hedge of long-term government bonds, both methods should produce accurate hedge ratios.

Hedging Effectiveness for Fixed-Income Securities by Sector (A)

Now let us extend the analysis of hedging effectiveness to other sectors of the fixed-income market and the other Treasury futures contracts.

We will take an 8 percent coupon issue as the reference bond for each maturity and credit class, and regress its price change on the price change of a financial futures contract that could be used to hedge it. The resulting hedge ratio will adjust for the differences in maturity and credit rating, as well as for the average amount of tailing that would have been required. Most importantly, it will incorporate a correction for basis risk between the futures contract and each particular sector of the fixed-income market. The R^2 from the regression will provide a measure of hedging effectiveness.

Tables 2-2, 2-3, and 2-4 contain the results of regressions involving different futures contracts, different segments of the cash market, and different hedging horizons. We analyze the three major Treasury securities futures that are most likely to be of importance to most institutional investors: Treasury bills, ten-year Treasury notes, and long-term Treasury bonds, looking at both the nearest contract to expiration (up until the fifteenth of the delivery month), and the second nearest contract.

The cash market prices for the 8 percent reference bonds are synthetic prices computed from the constant maturity yield series compiled by the Federal Reserve for Treasury issues and by Moody's for corporate bonds. That is, the actual bonds included in the sample change as time goes on to maintain the same average maturity in each group. We have simply taken the yield at each maturity and calculated what the price of an 8 percent coupon bond would be at that yield. The corporate bond series contain a mixture of maturities, all over twenty years, so we have arbitrarily assumed a maturity of twenty-five years for them.

Because the cash prices are based on groups of bonds, the coefficients are partially affected by diversification that takes place in a portfolio. There is relatively more slippage between the yield of a single issue and the specific cheapest to deliver bond underlying a futures contract than there is between portfolios containing a number of similar issues.

The data are drawn from Friday closing prices from the period 7 January 1983 through 26 October 1984. To capture the fact that the effects of basis risk depend on the length of the hedging period, we show factors for one-, two-, and four-week hedges.

These tables contain a great many numbers, so it is worthwhile to summarize to some extent what they show about hedging with these three financial futures contracts.

The coefficients, as we mentioned above, include both the effect of differing maturity and basis risk. The maturity adjustment tends to make h^* higher the longer the maturity of the cash instrument, since its interest rate sensitivity is larger. For a maturity close to that of the underlying instrument of the futures contract, h^* based only on yield

Table 2–2.　Hedge Regression Results for Treasury Bill Futures.

Cash security		Nearest future			Next nearest future		
		1-week	2-weeks	4-weeks	1-week	2-weeks	4-weeks
Treasury							
6-month	Coef.	.41	.46	.53	.51	.56	.57
bill	R^2	.47	.56	.59	.63	.75	.78
1-year	Coef.	.46	.50	.58	.61	.67	.68
note	R^2	.49	.51	.56	.73	.84	.87
2-year	Coef.	.76	.81	1.06	1.07	1.20	1.27
	R^2	.41	.39	.54	.69	.76	.90
3-year	Coef.	1.07	1.12	1.44	1.53	1.71	1.80
	R^2	.39	.37	.51	.69	.76	.91
5-year	Coef.	1.46	1.46	1.91	2.19	2.41	2.58
	R^2	.34	.30	.41	.66	.71	.85
10-year	Coef.	2.01	2.00	2.39	3.13	3.43	3.53
	R^2	.30	.25	.32	.63	.66	.78
20-year	Coef.	2.39	2.37	2.55	3.63	3.94	3.95
	R^2	.30	.27	.26	.60	.66	.72
30-year	Coef.	2.48	2.60	2.77	3.76	4.23	4.28
	R^2	.30	.29	.26	.60	.67	.72
Corporate							
AAA	Coef.	1.44	1.58	2.38	2.16	2.56	3.11
	R^2	.19	.19	.34	.38	.45	.66
AA	Coef.	1.31	1.47	1.64	1.96	2.32	2.60
	R^2	.24	.24	.23	.45	.52	.67
A	Coef.	.84	1.08	1.10	1.25	1.63	1.80
	R^2	.17	.19	.17	.32	.38	.51
BAA	Coef.	.79	1.07	1.30	1.27	1.77	1.88
	R^2	.17	.20	.22	.37	.49	.53

Note: Coef. and R^2 are the slope coefficient and R^2 from the regression $DP = a + bDF$, where DP is the change in the (synthetic) price for the reference bond in the specified class and DF is the change in the futures price.

Table 2–3.   Hedge Regression Results for Treasury Note Futures.

Cash security		Nearest future			Next nearest future		
		1-week	2-weeks	4-weeks	1-week	2-weeks	4-weeks
Treasury							
6-month	Coef.	.14	.13	.16	.13	.13	.15
bill	R^2	.57	.57	.68	.55	.56	.66
1-year	Coef.	.17	.18	.19	.17	.18	.19
note	R^2	.74	.75	.82	.73	.75	.80
2-year	Coef.	.33	.35	.37	.32	.35	.37
	R^2	.81	.86	.89	.81	.86	.88
3-year	Coef.	.48	.51	.53	.48	.51	.53
	R^2	.85	.90	.94	.85	.91	.94
5-year	Coef.	.72	.76	.80	.71	.76	.80
	R^2	.88	.92	.95	.89	.93	.95
10-year	Coef.	1.07	1.12	1.13	1.06	1.13	1.14
	R^2	.91	.93	.95	.92	.94	.95
20-year	Coef.	1.24	1.27	1.30	1.23	1.29	1.31
	R^2	.88	.91	.91	.89	.93	.92
30-year	Coef.	1.29	1.34	1.40	1.28	1.35	1.41
	R^2	.89	.89	.91	.89	.91	.92
Corporate							
AAA	Coef.	.75	.83	1.01	.75	.86	1.01
	R^2	.57	.63	.81	.58	.67	.81
AA	Coef.	.66	.73	.85	.66	.75	.86
	R^2	.64	.68	.83	.66	.71	.85
A	Coef.	.44	.53	.61	.44	.54	.61
	R^2	.50	.54	.70	.49	.56	.69
BAA	Coef.	.43	.55	.61	.43	.55	.60
	R^2	.55	.62	.64	.54	.63	.64

Note: See the note to Table 2–2.

sensitivity should be approximately 1.0. The exception is the T-bill contract since the futures price in that market is quoted as 100 minus the *annualized* Treasury bill rate. For example, if the yield fell by forty basis points, the futures price would rise by 0.40, even though

Table 2–4.   Hedge Regression Results for Treasury Bond Futures.

		Nearest future			Next nearest future		
Cash security		1-week	2-weeks	4-weeks	1-week	2-weeks	4-weeks
Treasury							
6-month	Coef.	.11	.11	.12	.11	.11	.12
bill	R^2	.54	.60	.64	.53	.59	.64
1-year	Coef.	.14	.15	.15	.13	.15	.15
note	R^2	.69	.77	.78	.69	.77	.77
2-year	Coef.	.25	.29	.29	.25	.29	.28
	R^2	.77	.86	.86	.77	.86	.85
3-year	Coef.	.37	.42	.41	.38	.42	.41
	R^2	.81	.90	.91	.81	.90	.90
5-year	Coef.	.56	.62	.62	.56	.62	.62
	R^2	.85	.91	.93	.85	.92	.93
10-year	Coef.	.85	.92	.90	.85	.92	.89
	R^2	.90	.92	.95	.91	.93	.96
20-year	Coef.	1.01	1.06	1.05	1.02	1.06	1.04
	R^2	.90	.93	.94	.92	.94	.95
30-year	Coef.	1.06	1.13	1.14	1.06	1.14	1.13
	R^2	.93	.94	.95	.94	.95	.96
Corporate							
AAA	Coef.	.60	.70	.81	.61	.71	.80
	R^2	.57	.66	.83	.59	.68	.83
AA	Coef.	.54	.61	.69	.54	.62	.68
	R^2	.66	.70	.88	.67	.71	.88
A	Coef.	.35	.44	.47	.35	.44	.47
	R^2	.49	.54	.66	.49	.55	.66
BAA	Coef.	.35	.45	.49	.35	.45	.48
	R^2	.54	.63	.67	.55	.63	.67

Note: See the note to Table 2–2.

the price of a three-month bill would only go up by one-quarter of that, 0.10. This means that h^* for a hedge using T-bill futures should be 4 times the coefficient shown in Table 2–2.

Basis risk has the effect of reducing the risk minimizing hedge ratio. The larger basis risk is as a fraction of total return variability, the smaller h^* will become. Therefore, for a specific futures contract, we expect h^* to be higher for maturities closer to its underlying asset and for longer holding periods. These patterns are confirmed in the results. In general, hedging effectiveness goes up as the cash market instrument becomes more similar in maturity and credit rating to the reference security of the futures contract, and as the length of the hedging period increases. Both of these results are as expected.

In the case of the Treasury bill contract, but not the other two, hedge effectiveness seems to be markedly higher for the next nearest futures than for the nearest to expiration. The near bill future did not seem to be a very effective hedge for any of these cash instruments, probably because it has an average maturity of only about 1½ months, which is substantially shorter than even the six-month cash bill.

Hedging effectiveness was quite high for the two longer maturity futures contracts in the Treasury securities market. Even a one-week hedge eliminated about 90 percent or more of the variance for government securities near to the maturity of the underlying instruments. Corporate bonds, however, were not so easy to hedge. Once the R^2 drops to the 0.6–0.7 range, basis risk is a significant factor that needs to be taken into account explicitly in designing a hedge.

The impact on the risk-minimizing hedge ratio is apparent when one compares the coefficients for twenty-five-year corporate bonds to those for the twenty- and thirty-year Treasuries with the same coupon. For example, a four-week hedge with the nearest futures had an h^* of 1.30 for a twenty-year 8 percent T-bond and 1.40 for one with thirty years to maturity. But the same hedge for an 8 percent twenty-five-year A-rated corporate issue called for a hedge ratio of only 0.61, less than half of the Treasury value.

We have seen that the theoretical hedge ratio for a long-term Treasury bond is quite close to the empirical estimate, while the empirical h^* for a corporate bond is only a fraction of the value for a comparable T-bond. It may be reasonable to use the ratio of these coefficients to deflate the theoretical hedge ratio estimated for a corporate bond hedge, in order to adjust approximately for its basis risk. But bear in mind that these relationships are estimated from data from a particular period in the past and may not continue to hold in the future, and they are based on aggregated data, so the adjustment for a hedge involving a single bond will be different.

SELECTING THE CONTRACT

In this section we will discuss the considerations to be weighed in choosing the futures contract, market, and month in which to trade.

An important question that needs to be addressed at the outset is whether the particular risk that the cash position is exposed to can be suitably hedged in the futures market at all. In some cases a financial futures contract may be available that is written on a cash instrument that is of the same type as the one being hedged, but quite frequently this will not be the case and only a cross-hedge using a future based on a different type of instrument will be available. If the position being hedged is undiversified — for example, a private placement of a single firm's debt securities — the impact of basis risk is magnified. Further, if the hedged position is to be held only a short period of time, basis risk becomes still greater. In some cases, the result will be that the amount of price risk that can be hedged is small relative to the basis risk that would be taken on by trading futures.

However, for investment grade bonds or similar types of loan contracts of more than a few years maturity, the existing futures contracts allow a reasonable amount of risk reduction in a properly designed hedge. In this case, a futures contract should be chosen that has in the past proved most closely correlated with the instrument being hedged. The main exception is if concern about liquidity in the market might shift the choice to another contract with higher liquidity but only second highest correlation.

Liquidity Concerns

An important factor that will enter in decisions about the choice of the contract is its "liquidity" — the ease with which a transaction can be executed without affecting the price level significantly. For example, a market in which an order of twenty contracts can be executed with no appreciable change in price from the previous transaction is considered to be quite liquid. In contrast, a market in which an order of two to five contracts cannot be executed without a significant impact on price is illiquid.

In thin (illiquid) contracts the effective bid-asked spread will usually be large. This spread is a major component of the cost of executing transactions on the floor of the exchange (which, in turn, is one of the major costs of hedging). Liquidity is particularly important when placing large orders. It should be possible for a hedger to remove his position without having to make a significant concession in price. A reasonable rule of thumb to use would be not to take a position greater than 20 percent of the average daily volume in any given contract month.

The need for a liquid market may even dictate the exchange on which to trade, in the case of duplicative contracts. In some cases, a hedger may find that a more satisfactory hedge can be achieved in a market that is a cross-hedge but which has active trading than in a thin market based on the security he wishes to hedge.

Selecting the Contract Month

Once the choice of the futures contract has been made and the hedge ratio has been determined, a remaining important decision is the choice of the contract months to establish the position. Although there are several basic strategies that can be employed with respect to this selection, two general approaches can be identified.

The first is the "portfolio" approach. The hedger who is faced with risk exposure at multiple points in time uses a portfolio of futures contracts such that their maturity months coincide with the end of his multiple hedging horizons. The second approach, which is more dynamic in character, can be called the "price relationship" approach. Here often a single contract month is used to put on the hedge, but based on a continuous study of the price structure that exists among the various futures contract months, positions are shifted into the more advantageous contracts and out of the less advantageous ones. For example, if the hedger expects the September contract to decrease in price at a faster rate than the March contract, he will put on short positions in the September contract rather than the March contract. Because it is a simpler strategy, suited to a hedger who is concerned primarily with risk reduction, we will concentrate on the portfolio approach here and defer most of the discussion of the price relationship approach until the next chapter.

The chief trade-off in the choice of the contract month for hedging a distant exposure is basis risk versus liquidity. By choosing a futures contract of approximately the same maturity as the exposure, the basis risk is minimized, but usually the liquidity in such a distant contract is low. On the other hand, in choosing a nearby contract the liquidity is high but the basis risk is also higher, due to the maturity mismatch and the need to roll the futures position over periodically as the nearby contracts expire.

Strategies for Hedges of Risk Exposure at More Than One Horizon (A)

Two basic strategies of contract month selection are discussed below for the case of a cash position with multiple risk exposure.

Strip Hedge

This is an example of the portfolio approach in contract month selection. In this relatively straightforward strategy, contracts are chosen at the outset such that the maturity of each futures instrument approximately matches the time span of the cash market risk exposure it is hedging.

Example: Assume that on 1 April a hedger is faced with the following multiple-point risk exposure. Holding a portfolio of $30,000,000 worth of three-month T-bills that have to be sold on 1 May, $28,000,000 worth of six-month T-bills which have to be sold on 1 August, and $26,000,000 worth of one-year T-bills (maturing on 1 December) that have to be sold on 1 November. His points of risk exposure are on 1 May, 1 August, and 1 November.

Adopting the portfolio approach and implementing a strip hedge, the hedger would buy thirty June T-bill futures, twenty-eight September T-bill futures, and twenty-six December T-bill futures on 1 April. On 1 May, he will sell the thirty June T-bill futures; on 1 August, he will sell the twenty-eight September T-bill futures; and finally on 1 November he will sell the remaining twenty-six December T-bill futures. Clearly, here each exposure is hedged with a futures contract with a delivery date just after the exposure date.

Rolling Hedge

If the liquidity in the more distant contracts is not adequate, the most common alternative to the above strategy is a *rolling hedge*. This hedge can also be viewed as an example of the portfolio approach in that different month contracts are held and used to hedge exposure at multiple points in time. However, to take advantage of the liquidity of the nearby contract, this strategy puts on the whole hedge amount in the nearby contract; as liquidity grows in the deferred contracts, the appropriate number of nearby contracts are rolled over into the more distant contracts.

Example: Let us consider again the risk exposure of the previous example. The rolling hedge strategy will be implemented as follows:

1 April	*1 May*	*1 August*	*1 November*
Buy 84 June T-bill futures	Sell 84 June T-bill futures; buy 54 Sept T-bill futures	Sell 54 Sept T-bill futures; buy 26 December T-bill futures	Sell 26 December T-bill futures

This hedge takes advantage of the higher liquidity of the nearby contracts, without exposing the portfolio to too much basis risk.

The above have been relatively conservative hedging strategies in that they do not attempt to take any advantage of the structure of futures prices that may offer opportunities for more favorable terms in the hedge. A more sophisticated hedging strategy can entail continual reevaluation of the price structure among contract months and shifting positions to contracts offering the most advantageous relative price. For example, if the hedger expects the December contract to decrease in price at a faster rate than the June contract, he is better off putting on short positions in the December contract rather than the June contract. We will have more to say about futures pricing and opportunities for reducing the cost of hedging in the next chapter.

RESIDUAL RISK IN A HEDGED POSITION

We have devoted considerable time to describing how a futures hedge works to reduce the exposure of a cash market position to the risk of price fluctuations. In the last section of this chapter we will discuss the types of risk that a futures hedge cannot eliminate. One reason for doing this is to address directly the concerns of many institutional investors who have had no experience with futures and continue to view them as a risky proposition, despite their value in hedging. The risks we will consider are basis risk, estimation risk, credit risk, risk arising from marking to market in futures, and the risk of manipulation in the futures market.

One of the most apparent risks remaining in a hedged position is basis risk, which we have talked about in detail already. Except under very specific circumstances, a futures hedge will be exposed to some risk that the values of the cash position being hedged and the futures contract will not change exactly together over time. When the hedge is lifted, it is possible that an adverse change in the basis will have occurred, leading to a loss or at least a lower return than anticipated. Since basis risk is an inherent part of futures hedging, it is essential that it be understood and taken into account properly in designing the hedge strategy. This is done in two ways. First, the hedger must recognize the cases in which basis risk is likely to play a relatively larger role. These are hedges in which (1) the cash item being hedged is quite different in credit rating, maturity or type from the underlying security for the futures contract (e.g., a hedge of a twelve-year mortgage with T-bond futures); (2) the cash item is a single issue rather than a portfolio of similar issues, especially if the cash market is not very liquid (e.g., a hedge of a single corporate bond issue from a small A-rated firm); (3) the expected duration of the hedge is short (e.g., one week or less). Each of these factors adds basis risk, so that if they are present in combination, basis risk can become a serious problem. Some cash market risks are just not suitable candidates for hedging, and in such cases it is possible for an inaccurately designed "hedge" actually to increase risk.

The second principle in dealing with basis risk is that the larger basis risk is expected to be, the smaller should be the hedge ratio, because exposure to basis risk increases with the size of the futures position taken. Recalling the risk-return trade-off in a hedged position that was displayed in Figure 2–1, one can see that for a short hedge, overhedging is a more serious mistake than underhedging. Since hedging reduces both risk and expected return, reducing the scale of the hedge permits higher risk but also higher returns along with it. Hedging too much, by contrast, can push the position past the point of minimum risk into the region where expected return continues to drop but risk is increasing. When in doubt about the extent of basis risk, it is better to err on the side of having too small a futures position than one too large.

The appropriate response to basis risk in a long hedge is less clear. As we will discuss in the next chapter, a long futures contract on a risky security should have a positive expected return. That means that expected return should go up as more futures are purchased even if one goes beyond the point of minimum risk. However, this increase in expected returns would be essentially due to the reward offered by a competitive market to those who take on extra risk. In other words, it is the expected return to speculation in the futures market. Depending on the particulars of the hedge strategy being followed, the hedger may be in the fortunate position of being able to earn this return at the same time he is reducing his particular risk, as when a long hedge is used to hedge a short position in the cash market. Or he may be effectively increasing his risk, as when an anticipatory long hedge allows the hedger to lock in a purchase price and to take on the risk today of securities he will actually buy only at a later time. In any case, prudence dictates that for both long and short hedges, overhedging is to be avoided.

Estimation risk is related to basis risk and has the same remedy. The problem is that estimating h^* from past data or deducing it from assumptions about the probable price relationship between the position being hedged and the futures contract will always produce a hedge ratio that is subject to estimation error. It is a problem that the hedger must be aware of, so that he does not put an inappropriate amount of confidence in the exact number his procedure for estimating the hedge ratio produces. As with basis risk, the cost of overhedging can be substantially more severe than the cost of underhedging. Uncertainty about the precise value of h^* should lead one to reduce the scale of the hedge amount.

A different type of risk is credit risk. What is the chance that the opposite party in a financial transaction will default? One of the great advantages of an organized futures market over a forward market, which offers many of the same opportunities for hedging, is that futures contracts are guaranteed by the exchange Clearing House. Financial integrity of the contracts does not depend upon the creditworthiness of the opposite party to the futures trade the way it does in a forward market. Thus there is virtually no risk that the futures contract will not ultimately be fulfilled. There is, however, the possibility in some types of transactions that default on a commitment in the cash market will cause more serious repercussions in a hedged position than in an unhedged position, because the futures contracts remain binding on the hedger even if his cash position has changed. For example, if a life insurance company were to make a forward loan commitment at a prespecified interest rate, which it then hedged in the futures market by selling Treasury bond futures, it would be exposed to a default risk on its cash market position. If interest rates fell during the commitment period and the borrower defaulted on his obligation to take down the loan, in addition to the opportunity loss of not being able to make the loan at the rate agreed upon, there would be an actual loss on the short bond futures position for which the company was still liable. If this type of risk is present, once again reducing the scale of the hedge is appropriate.

A different type of risk uniquely associated with futures trading arises from the practice of marking to market.

Marking a futures position to market does not alter the aggregate amount of cash paid to settle a long position or received in settlement of a short position; it simply changes the timing of the cash flow. However, for a hedger this can have significant consequences if he is hedging the value of a cash position that does not generate cash flows before the end of the holding period. Institutions need to be aware that, although they are operating what they see as a fully hedged position, they may be required to put up considerable sums of margin during the life of the hedge as their futures are marked to market while their cash position is not. To avoid liquidity problems, it is important for a hedger to assess the impact of possible adverse variation margin flows and maintain a sufficient fund of liquid assets as a part of a well-planned hedging program. We will discuss how such a fund should be set up below in Chapter 7.

A final area of potential concern to hedgers is the possibility of manipulation or, more generally, artificial prices in the futures market. Two of the most serious problems of this type are corners and squeezes. A corner occurs when an investor or a group of investors gains sufficient control over the deliverable supply of the financial instrument or commodity that he is in a position to force holders of short futures positions to settle at high prices because they are not able to obtain the securities to make delivery. A squeeze is a similar situation in which the deliverable supply is restricted relative to the quantity required to make delivery in the futures market, but often for reasons other than direct manipulation. For example, if the Congress is unable to pass an increase in the debt ceiling in time for the Treasury to issue the T-bills that would be delivered against a maturing T-bill futures contract, a squeeze could develop.

Corners are illegal, and limits on the maximum size of futures positions, along with extensive surveillance of the marketplace by the exchanges and the Commodity Futures Trading Commission, make the possibility of a successful corner extremely remote. However, squeezes are possible in certain circumstances. Such problems can arise in poorly designed contracts that specify the deliverable instrument very narrowly. For the markets we have been discussing, the significant outstanding dollar amount of deliverable instruments makes it an unlikely situation. For example, the T-bond and T-note futures contracts allow a wide range of deliverable bonds. Most short-term interest rate contracts also specify a range of deliverable instruments. Finally, in contracts like stock index futures, use of cash settlement eliminates the problem.

3 THE PRICING OF FINANCIAL FUTURES CONTRACTS

This chapter describes the relationship between the price of a futures contract and the price in the relevant cash market. Understanding this relationship is important for optimal use of futures in hedging because it is what determines the cost of risk reduction. Also, in the last chapter we mentioned a more sophisticated approach to the selection of contract and contract month that involved studying the price structure among the various futures contracts and the cash instruments in order to optimize the choice of hedging vehicle according to whether a particular contract was currently overpriced or underpriced. Clearly, the notion of a "fair" or "theoretical" price for a futures contract is needed to provide the appropriate benchmark for identifying underpriced and overpriced contracts if they exist. Finally, observed futures prices can provide information that can be valuable to an issuer in setting the terms of cash instruments it is selling.

The underlying principle that is used in calculating a theoretical price for a futures contract is arbitrage. Arbitrage should force any two securities, or portfolios of securities, that are perfect substitutes to sell for the same price. For example, on the futures delivery date a futures contract can be converted to the underlying cash instrument, so its price must be the same. The futures price "converges" at maturity to the adjusted price (i.e., adjusting for any delivery factor that would be applied) of the cheapest deliverable cash instrument. Because of this, prior to delivery, the futures contract will also have a well-defined relationship to the underlying cash instrument, which is known as the cost of carry relation.

THE COST OF CARRY RELATION

The cost of carry concept asserts that the futures price should reflect the current cash price for the underlying security plus the net cost of carrying it until the futures delivery date.

$$\text{Futures Price} = \text{Spot Price} + \text{Net Carrying Costs}$$
$$F = P + c. \tag{3.1}$$

In equation (3.1) and throughout this chapter, except where noted explicitly, the spot price P will be taken to mean the actual price of a cash market security *adjusted by its delivery factor* in order to express it in the same terms as the futures price. For example, for the Treasury bond contract $P = $ (actual price)/(delivery factor).

This relationship is based on the following arbitrage trade. Consider buying the appropriate quantity of the deliverable instrument in the cash market, financing the purchase at the current short term borrowing rate, and selling a futures contract to lock in the price that the security can be sold for on the delivery date. Then suppose the position is held until the futures mature, at which time the securities are delivered against the futures contract. Since the futures contract fixes the liquidation value of the position, the transaction is essentially riskless. And assuming the entire trade is financed by borrowing at the short-term interest rate, there is no net investment. Thus, unless the cost of setting this position up by buying the cash securities and carrying them is exactly equal to the futures price, there will be a riskless profit that could be earned by an arbitrageur with no net investment of capital.

Rearranging equation (3.1) allows us to express the same relation in terms of the basis, the futures price minus the cash price: $F - P = B = c$. The basis should simply be equal to the net cost of carry. If the basis were greater than c, arbitrageurs would buy spot, sell futures, and hold until delivery to earn an arbitrage profit equal to $F - P - c$. If, on the other hand, $F - P$ is less than c, they would do the opposite: sell spot, invest the proceeds in riskless securities, and buy futures. If

Table 3-1.   Closing Prices for Silver Futures 31 December 1984.

Contract	Price
JAN	636.5
FEB	641.5
APR	651.0
JUN	661.5
AUG	672.5
OCT	684.0
DEC	696.0
Spot price	628.8

the arbitrage worked perfectly, it would ensure that the futures price would always equal the cash price plus the cost of carry—that is, $F = P + c$.

The prices of metal futures present one of the simplest examples of cost of carry pricing. Table 3-1 shows closing prices for silver futures on the COMEX on the last trading day in 1984. Two things are apparent in these prices: (1) The futures prices are higher than the cash price, and (2) the longer the maturity of the futures contract (i.e., the more delayed the delivery date is), the higher the price. This is consistent with the cost of carry concept, since the net carrying cost to buy the metal and keep it until delivery largely consists of the interest expense on the funds tied up by the purchase, plus a relatively small amount for insurance, storage costs, and assay expenses. The more delayed the delivery date, the greater is the interest cost, so F is greater than P by an amount that increases with the maturity of the futures contract.

The same principle applies to interest rate futures. Here, however, net carrying cost is the (opportunity) cost of funds, minus any cash inflows from coupon interest on the cash instrument.

The conventional borrowing method for Treasury securities is a repurchase agreement—often called a "repo" or "RP"—in which the security itself is used as collateral for the loan. For example, when an arbitrageur purchases Treasury bonds valued at $1 million in the cash market, he typically obtains the $1 million by putting them out on repurchase. That is, he sells them under an agreement to repurchase them on a future date at today's price plus interest on the loan. Most repurchase agreements are overnight loans, but they can generally be rolled over (at what may be a different repo rate) the following day. That is, the repurchase date is on demand. Term repurchases, maturing on an agreed upon date further in the future, are also possible but not always so easy to arrange.

While the arbitrageur must pay interest on the loan at the prevailing repo rate, he accrues interest on the bonds at the same time. When interest income exceeds cost of carry interest expense, the arbitrageur enjoys "positive carry" or net interest income. The opposite case is called "negative carry" and describes the situation when interest expense for carrying the position is greater than interest income on the long-term asset.

A complication arises when a variety of cash securities are deliverable against the futures contract. The reference bond for the CBT T-bond futures contract has an 8 percent coupon and twenty years to maturity, but any T-bond with a minimum of fifteen years to maturity or first call is deliverable. As we described in Chapter 2, the invoice price paid on delivery is adjusted for the bond's coupon and maturity characteristics using a conversion factor based on price maintenance (i.e., the price of the bond at which it yields 8 percent, divided by face value). This option introduces the consideration of which among the deliverable bonds is the "cheapest to deliver."

Although the conversion factor seems like it ought to put all bonds on an equal footing, so that one deliverable bond would be as good as another, this is not the case for the T-bond contract or for more than a handful of other futures contracts. Two factors act to make one, or in some cases a small number of bonds, clearly cheaper to deliver than others. The conversion factor is designed to make every bond equally attractive for delivery, when all are yielding 8 percent. But in general, differences in coupon and maturity cause different bonds to trade in the cash market at different yields. If an 8 percent twenty-year bond is currently priced to yield 8 percent, some other bond, say a 14 percent thirty-year issue, will be priced at a higher yield. Applying the conversion factor based on an 8 percent yield will lead to a lower adjusted price for the 14 percent bond than for the 8 percent bond.

Secondly, the conversion factor gives the appropriate ratio of the costs of $100,000 face value of the bond in question relative to the reference bond only at a yield of 8 percent. As market yields move away from 8 percent, bond values will change at different rates. As we will discuss in detail in Chapter 5, how much a bond's price changes with a given change in yield depends on its "duration." A bond with a higher duration will drop in value faster than the 8 percent reference bond when yields go up. This means that at the same yield, the cost of $100,000 face value of the high duration bond relative to the reference bond will be less than the conversion factor, and it will be cheaper to deliver. For this reason, as long as market yields are above 8 percent, typically it is the bond with the highest duration that is cheapest to deliver against the T-bond or T-note contract, although yield differences in the market for different bonds can alter this.

Thus, the relevant spot price P to use in computing the theoretical futures price is the cash price of the cheapest bond to deliver divided by the conversion factor. The date to which one counts accrued interest on the purchase price of the bond, and from which one computes the financing cost until future expiration, is the settlement date for the bond purchase. This is one business day after the transaction date.

$$c = \frac{1}{D}\left[(P+A)\left(r\frac{T}{360}\right) - Y\frac{T}{365}\right], \qquad (3.2)$$

where c is the net carrying cost,
D is the bond's delivery factor,
P is the current cash price of the cheapest deliverable instrument,
A is accrued interest up to cash settlement day since the last coupon payment date,
r is the cost of funds, assumed to be quoted on the basis of a 360-day year (e.g., the overnight repo rate),
T is the number of days from settlement date to futures expiration, and
Y is the annual coupon on the cash instrument.

A detailed example will illustrate how this equation is used.

Pricing Treasury Bond Futures off the Cheapest to Deliver Bond: An Example

Let us take the CBT June 1985 T-bond futures contract. We can determine a theoretical price for the contract on, say, 17 May 1985 by examining the prices of deliverable bonds available on that day and considering the relevant carrying costs.

The cheapest deliverable bond against the T-bond contract under consideration will be the one for which the theoretical futures price derived by the procedure we are about to describe is lowest. Normally it is the deliverable bond with the highest duration.

Another way to know which is the cheapest deliverable bond is that it is the one with the highest implied repo rate, as will be described below. But the simplest way to find out the correct bond is simply to ask any government bond dealer or futures commission merchant.

Table 3-2 shows the deliverable bonds for the June 1985 Treasury bond futures contract and the theoretical futures price that would correspond to each if it were cheapest to deliver. We also show the implied repo rates and durations for the deliverable bonds.

We see that the 7⅝ of February 2007 is cheapest to deliver, with a theoretical futures price of 74.13 (74⁴⁄₃₂). That figure is derived as follows.

Table 3-2.   Deliverable Bonds for June 1985 Treasury Bond Futures as of 17 May 1985.

Bond		Price	Delivery Factor	Theo-retical Future	Implied Repo Rate	Duration
7⅝	2007	71.781	0.9660	74.13	3.83	9.16
11¼	2015	101.594	1.3661	74.13	3.64	9.13
7⅞	2007	73.469	0.9882	74.14	3.55	9.18
12½	2014	110.188	1.4769	74.37	0.94	8.64
10⅜	2012	92.969	1.2448	74.44	−0.17	9.06
12	2013	105.938	1.4177	74.49	−0.47	8.59
8¾	2008	80.000	1.0711	74.46	−0.44	9.06
8⅜	2008	77.406	1.0355	74.55	−1.29	9.14
11¾	2014	104.594	1.3985	74.54	−1.37	8.61
9⅛	2009	83.000	1.1081	74.67	−2.98	9.03
13¼	2014	116.563	1.5541	74.74	−3.82	8.57
10	2010	90.344	1.1967	75.26	−10.01	8.99
10⅜	2009	93.031	1.2310	75.33	−10.88	8.88
14	2011	121.625	1.6080	75.36	−11.28	8.25
13⅞	2011	120.531	1.5898	75.54	−13.39	8.21
12¾	2010	111.688	1.4722	75.60	−14.06	8.25
11¾	2010	104.563	1.3672	76.24	−20.88	8.30

Note: Prices are intraday quotes from 5/17/85.

The current price of the bond is $P = 71^{25}/_{32} = 71.78125$.

The coupon is $Y = 7^{5}/_{8} = 7.625$, paid last on 2/15/85. Since settlement day is 5/20/85, the bond will have ninety-four days of accrued interest. $A = (94/365)(7.625) = 1.96$.

The current repurchase rate for Treasury securities is $r = 8.00\%$, and there are $T = 39$ days from settlement date until futures expiration date on 6/28/85.

Finally the delivery factor for this bond is 0.9660, which can be computed by finding the present value of the coupon payments and maturity value (per dollar of face value) discounted at 8 percent. Conversion factors are also available in tabular form in "Treasury Bond Futures Conversion Factors," published by the Financial Publishing Company of Boston, Massachusetts.

Plugging these figures into the cost of carry equation (3.2) gives

$$c = \frac{1}{0.9660}\left[(71.78+1.96)\left(0.08\frac{39}{360}\right)-7.625\frac{39}{365}\right]$$

$$= \frac{1}{0.9660}(0.639-0.815)$$

$$= -0.18.$$

The cost of carrying these bonds from the settlement date until futures expiration is negative since they pay more in coupon yield than the cost of financing the purchase at the repurchase rate.

The theoretical futures price F^e can now be obtained using equation (3.1), after adjusting the cash price by the delivery factor:

$$F^e = \frac{P}{D}+c$$

$$= \frac{71.78}{0.9660}-0.18$$

$$= 74.13.$$

This price is close but not equal to the futures price of $73^{25}/_{32} = 73.7813$. Possible reasons for the discrepancy include the following.
1. A tacit assumption in our calculation is that the cash instrument that is cheapest to deliver when assessed on 17 May 1985 is expected to remain so on the delivery date. It is possible that some other bond could be anticipated to become cheapest-to-deliver within the next thirty-nine days.

2. The accuracy of the repo rate might be questioned. In principle, the term repo rate representing the actual number of days until delivery should be used in this calculation rather than the overnight repo rate. Financing with overnight repos involves risk, since it requires continually rolling the loan over at rates that can change from day to day. However, because long-term repos are frequently difficult to arrange, most arbitrageurs would finance in the overnight market and simply bear the risk from short-term rate movements. The cost of funds should actually be the *expected average* repo rate over the holding period.

3. The delivery date on a long futures contract could be any business day in the delivery month. This could lengthen or shorten the holding period. Further, the seller has a variety of other delivery options that favor the short side of the futures market over the long. Taking account of the economic value of the delivery options should cause the futures to sell somewhat below the cost of carry level we have calculated. We feel that it is the value of these options that accounts for the bulk of the price discrepancy we found, and for the fact that the futures price is normally several thirty-seconds below its theoretical cost of carry value.

4. Transactions costs such as commissions, the cost of maintaining the necessary margin on deposit, and so on, and market inefficiencies (to the extent that they exist) will also affect the reliability of the theoretical value we have derived. The existence of transactions costs leads to a range around the theoretical price within which arbitrage is not profitable. As long as the actual price lies within the transactions cost bounds, arbitrage to drive it exactly to its theoretical value need not occur.

The Pattern of Futures Prices

This relationship provides several insights about the concurrent price of the cash instrument and the futures contract. For example, when the yield curve is positively sloped, with short-term rates lower than long-term rates as they were here, the net cost of carry will be negative (i.e., the long bonds would yield more than the cost of borrowing to finance the bond purchase). Saying this another way, the *return* to carrying long-term securities financed at the short-term rate is positive. In somewhat confusing terminology, this situation is often referred to as a "positive carry" market. In a positive carry market, futures prices will be lower than the cash price, and futures for more

Table 3-3.   Treasury Bond Futures Prices on 14 November 1984.

DEC	70-05
MAR 85	69-12
JUN	68-23
SEP	68-05
DEC	67-22
MAR 86	67-09
JUN	66-30
SEPT	66-20

distant delivery will be lower the further in the future delivery is. This pattern, which Keynes called "normal backwardation," can be seen in the futures price quotations for 15 November 1984 as shown in Table 3-3.

On the other hand, when the yield curve is negatively sloped, with short-term rates higher than long-term rates, the net cost of carry will be positive. Because the return to carrying securities financed at the short-term rate is negative, this is also called a negative carry market. Since the net cost of carry "c" is positive and increasing in the time to delivery, our equation (3.1) implies that $F - P$ should be positive and increasing for contracts of more delayed delivery. In other words, futures contracts should be priced higher than the cash price, and the longer the maturity of the futures contract, the higher the price. This pattern of futures prices is called "contango." Notice that in both cases it is actually *coupon* yield, not yield to maturity, that determines whether the net cost of carry is positive or negative.

In the same way that a theoretical futures price can be derived from the current spot price of the cheapest deliverable instrument, the theoretical spread between futures prices for different delivery months can be determined from the same relation. This is done simply by replacing the cash price P in equation (3.2) by $F_t D$, where F_t is the futures price for month t expiration, to get the cost of carry from one futures expiration date to the next. The resulting c is then the theoretical spread between the two futures prices.

The Implied Repo Rate

The above discussion has shown that one cannot use the futures market to obtain an independent reading on investors' expectations about future securities prices, much as it would be very useful to have one. However, one *can* derive information from the structure of futures prices regarding the expected future cost of carry. For financial instruments with known coupon payments or dividends, this amounts to an estimate of the cost of short-term funds in the future. Arbitrage between cash bills and futures keeps prices closely in line in both markets.

In using the cost of carry relationship [equations (3.1) and (3.2)] we took the existing repo rate as the cost of funds r to determine a theoretical value for the price of a futures contract. Using the same relationship we can ask the related question: For what value of the repo rate will the theoretical futures price equal the actual market price of the futures contract? The answer to this question is the *implied repo rate*. In equation (3.2), the implied repo rate (IRR) is the value of r that makes $c = F - P/D$. Solving for it gives

$$IRR = \left(\frac{360}{T}\right)\left(\frac{1}{P+A}\right)\left(DF - P + Y\frac{T}{365}\right). \qquad (3.3)$$

Example: The price of the June 1985 CBT T-bond futures contract on 17 May 1985 was $73\,{}^{25}\!/_{32}$ and the cheapest deliverable bond has been determined to be the $7\,{}^{5}\!/_{8}$ percent T-bond maturing in 2007 with a cash price of $71\,{}^{25}\!/_{32}$, and other characteristics are given above. Using equation (3.3) to determine the implied repo rate yields

$$IRR = \left(\frac{360}{39}\right)\left(\frac{1}{71.78 + 1.96}\right)\left[(0.9660 \times 73.78) - 71.78 + 7.625\frac{39}{365}\right]$$

$$= \left(\frac{360}{39}\right)\left(\frac{0.306}{73.74}\right) = 0.0383$$

$$= 3.83\%.$$

The implied repo rate is 3.83 percent. When the actual repo rate is higher, as was the case in the example, the theoretical futures price will be above the actual value.

The implied repo rate is the financing rate that would make the return on the strategy of borrowing at IRR, buying the cash securities, and hedging them in the futures market exactly zero. Another way of saying this is that the IRR is the riskless rate of return that would be earned on the "cash and carry" trade without borrowing to finance it. Therefore, the difference between the IRR and the actual repo rate is the excess return that would be earned by the arbitrage at current prices. In this case, the cash and carry arbitrage would earn $3.83 - 8.00 = -417$ basis points. Since this would result in a loss, the arbitrage needs to be reversed. One must sell short the cash bonds, invest the proceeds in the repo market at 8.00 percent, and *buy* futures in order to earn the 417 basis point arbitrage profit. Since this is a more difficult transaction than the cash and carry arbitrage, and more risky because one cannot control what will get delivered or when, it is not too surprising to find that the market has not arbitraged away this apparent profit opportunity.

EXPECTATIONS AND FUTURE INTEREST RATES IN THE STRUCTURE OF FUTURES PRICES

The cost of carry model is based on the principle of arbitrage, which is a strong foundation. But many people believe that the futures price reflects not carrying costs but price expectations in the market. In this section, we will first discuss the role of expectations in futures price formation. We will then go on to describe the interaction between the structure of futures prices and future short-term interest rates.

The Role of Expectations

An alternative model of the relationship between the futures price and the cash market price can be stated in terms of the expectations of the market participants (hedgers, speculators, and arbitrageurs). This model states that the current futures price is equal to the market's expected value of the spot price of the cash instrument *on delivery date*.

$$F = E(P_T), \tag{3.4}$$

where $E(P_T)$ is the market's expectation of the spot price on delivery date.

The rationale for this relationship is that the futures market is composed of a large number of rational traders who base their trading on their expectations about the value of the contracts. If a majority of them felt that the spot price at maturity would be above the current futures price, they would buy, driving futures up. Similarly, whenever the bulk of the market population believed that prices would drop by expiration, they would sell short and precipitate the decline immediately. The only equilibrium with supply exactly matching demand, it is argued, will be when the futures price is exactly equal to the market's average expectation for the spot price at expiration.

While this argument seems plausible, and it has been offered widely as an explanation of price determination in futures markets, it is important to recognize that it is inconsistent with the arbitrage-based cost of carry model that we have been discussing. If the futures price is set by the cost of carry, then it is not the market's expectation of the future spot price at the expiration of the futures contract. And if the futures price is the expected value of the future spot price, then it is not being determined by the cost of carry. Which model, then, is true?

The cost of carry model is the correct explanation of futures price determination, for the most part. The problem with the reasoning behind the expectations view is that it does not take proper account of hedging and arbitrage. Consider what anyone holding a position in Treasury bonds that could be delivered against the T-bond contract would do if the futures price were equal to the price he expected to prevail in the cash market at expiration. He would sell futures against his cash bonds, expecting to get exactly the same return as if he did not hedge but eliminating all of the risk. Since risky long-term bonds are expected to yield more than riskless short-term assets, this strategy would offer a higher riskless return than was available on other riskless investments, and all sensible investors should rush to take advantage of it. As long as the expected return to this cash and carry arbitrage was above the repurchase rate, there would be arbitrage trading driving cash prices for deliverable bonds up and futures prices down, until the cost of carry relation, equation (3.1), held in the market.

There are, however, a few exceptions and subtleties to the rule. Most important is the misconception (which we abetted somewhat in the previous paragraphs) that under the cost of carry model, futures prices do not involve the market's expectation of the price of the cash instrument on the futures delivery date at all. They do incorporate the expected future cash price but only insofar as it is embodied in the current cash price. Clearly, the current market price for any security depends on the market's expectation of what it will be worth in the future, compared with alternative investments that could be made.

A security should be priced in the market so that it is expected to earn a fair rate of return commensurate with its risk over any investment horizon, including the period from now until the expiration of the futures contract. The point of the cost of carry model is that *given the current cash price,* expectations about the cash price at expiration should not have any *independent* effect on futures prices.

A second point with respect to expectations is that they can play a role in futures pricing when the arbitrage process is restricted by transactions costs or other problems, such as difficulty in selling short in the cash market. Such problems with doing the cash and carry arbitrage are present to some extent in all markets. We described above how transactions costs create a band within which the futures price can fluctuate without giving rise to arbitrage. Where the futures price will lie within this band can be influenced by market expectations (to the extent that they differ from the expectations of participants in the cash market who are setting prices there). If the market believes that the cash price will be higher in the future, the futures price will rise to the upper end of its range, while if lower prices are anticipated, it can be pushed below its theoretical level. Arbitrage in futures for Treasury securities is relatively straightforward for the bond dealers and other major participants in the cash market, so the arbitrage bounds are fairly tight in those markets, and the scope for expectations-based price fluctuation is limited. In the stock index futures contracts, which we will discuss below in Chapter 6, arbitrage is a great deal more difficult, and deviations from the cost of carry prices are common and can be quite large.

Forward Rates and Treasury Bill Futures Prices (A)

The Treasury bill futures market presents a special case, since the T-bill rate is itself a measure of the riskless cost of funds. The implied repo rate in bill futures is essentially the forward T-bill rate, which is directly comparable to the forward rate implied by cash bill prices. Arbitrage between cash bills and futures keeps prices closely in line in both markets.

We will consider a general model relating the theoretical price of a T-bill futures contract to the current and forward rates available in the cash market. Consider the pricing of a futures contract maturing t_1 days from now written on an underlying instrument, say, a T-bill maturing t_2 days after that — for instance, a futures contract maturing in forty-five days ($t_1 = 45$) written on a ninety-one-day T-bill ($t_2 = 91$). Now consider the two options that an investor has: (1) Invest in a T-bill of maturity ($t_1 + t_2$); or (2) invest in a t_1-day bill, and buy a futures contract maturing in t_1 days written on a t_2-day bill.

Since a Treasury bill is a discount instrument making a single payment of 100 (100 percent of par) at maturity, the total return over the holding period to maturity is just $1 + R = 100/P$. The first strategy has a total return therefore of $100/P(t_1 + t_2)$, where $P(t_1 + t_2)$ is the price of the ($t_1 + t_2$)-day bill.

The second strategy involves a t_1-day bill plus a rollover into a second bill that will be delivered against the futures contract in t_1 days. Both strategies allow an investor to fix the return on a ($t_1 + t_2$) riskless instrument, so these two strategies must offer equivalent returns or there would be an arbitrage opportunity. Therefore,

$$\frac{100}{P(t_1 + t_2)} = \left(\frac{100}{P(t_1)}\right)\left(\frac{100}{P_F}\right), \tag{3.5}$$

where P_F is the price of the bill that will be purchased at maturity of the futures contract. (This is not F, the futures price, due to the pricing convention used for T-bill futures.)

Equivalently, this equation can be written

$$1 + R_2 = (1 + R_1)(1 + f_2), \tag{3.6}$$

where R_1 and R_2 are total returns on the t_1- and ($t_1 + t_2$)-day bills and f_2 is the implied *forward* rate (expressed as a total return) on a t_2-day bill valid t_1 days from now. The corresponding bond equivalent bill yield r_{f2} is given by

$$r_{f2} = 100\left(\frac{365}{t_2}\right)f_2. \tag{3.7}$$

Solving (3.5) for P_F gives

$$P_F = 100[P(t_1 + t_2)/P(t_1)]. \tag{3.8}$$

To avoid arbitrage between cash bills and futures, P_F should be the invoice price of the bill that would be delivered against the futures contract. Given the pricing convention used by the International Monetary Market for Treasury bill futures (as well as for Eurodollar and Domestic CD futures), the theoretical price should be

$$F = 100 - (100 - P_F)(360/t_2). \tag{3.9}$$

Example: Let us use equations (3.8) and (3.9) to determine the price of an IMM March 1985 contract, as of 15 November 1984 if the deliverable bill against the futures contract is the 21 June 1985 T-bill (bid yield 8.94, asked yield 8.86, average of 8.90; as read from *Wall Street Journal* quotations of 15 November 1984). We can use the following steps to determine the theoretical futures price F:

1. Determine the T-bill rate applicable from the current date to the delivery date of the futures contract $-t_1$ days as given in the general formulation. For the period between 15 November 1984 and the Thursday of the third week of March (21 March 1985), this period is 127 days. The T-bill maturing 21 March 1985, from the *Wall Street Journal* of 15 November 1984, has a bid yield 8.72 and ask yield 8.69.

2. Compute the numbers $P(t_1 + t_2) = P(217 \text{ days})$ and $P(t_1) = P(127 \text{ days})$ from the average quoted prices of the respective T-bills. P_F is then given by (3.8).

$$P_F = 100 \frac{100 - 8.90(217/360)}{100 - 8.70(127/360)}$$

$$= 100 \frac{94.64}{96.93}$$

$$= 97.63.$$

3. Now, F, the price of the futures contract as it is conventionally quoted, is given by the equation (3.9).

$$F = 100 - [100 - 97.63(360/90)]$$

$$= 100 - 9.48$$

$$= 90.52.$$

Again, looking at the *Wall Street Journal* quotations, we find that the IMM March 1985 T-bill contracts had a settlement price of 90.89. This is close, though not exact.

Bounds on the Theoretical Pricing Relationship (A)

A final comment on this theoretical pricing relationship is in order. As we have mentioned, transactions costs (brokerage costs, bid-ask spreads, and the costs of providing initial and maintenance margins) and limitations or restrictions on available strategies (e.g., no short sales of the cash security are allowed) would cause the theoretical values to deviate from the actual prices. Bounds for the futures price can sometimes be worked out, incorporating the effect of transactions costs and restrictions on trading. For example, equation (3.8), which assumes no commission costs and no bid-ask spread, can be modified as follows, assuming a round-trip commission of $20 on a $1 million face value contract (i.e., 0.00002 per dollar of face value).

To prevent arbitrage the futures price must be such that it is neither worthwhile to buy the long maturity bill, sell the short maturity bill and sell futures, nor to sell the long bill and buy the short bill and futures. This bounds the theoretical futures price as follows:

$$\frac{P^B(t_1+t_2)}{P^A(t_1)} - 0.00002 \le \frac{P_F}{100} \le \frac{P^A(t_1+t_2)}{P^B(t_1)} + 0.00002, \qquad (3.10)$$

where the superscripts A and B denote the ask and bid prices respectively.

From their stated yields, the bid and ask prices for these bills are

$$P^A(217) = 94.66$$

$$P^B(217) = 94.61$$

$$P^A(127) = 96.93$$

$$P^B(127) = 96.92$$

From (3.10) the bounds on P_F are

$$97.60 \le P_F \le 97.67.$$

The above range on P_F can be written in terms of a range on F, the futures price quoted in terms of the IMM index, using equation (3.9):

$$90.42 \le F \le 90.66.$$

FUTURES PRICING AND THE COST OF HEDGING

Since the return on a hedged position is just the return on the securities held unhedged plus the return on the futures contracts that are traded, one of the primary determinants of hedging performance is what return is earned on the futures component of the trade. In this section we will first discuss what return should be anticipated on a futures contract when it is correctly priced and how that is incorporated into the total expected return on the hedged position. We will then go on to discuss the causes of variation in this return and methods for dealing with it.

The Expected Return on Futures and on Futures Hedges

When futures contracts are priced according to the cost of carry model, the total return to a fully hedged position in the underlying cash securities is equal to the short-term riskless interest rate. In order to produce this return, the capital gain (or loss) that is locked in by selling futures, plus the yield that will be earned from coupon income during the holding period, must equal the riskless rate. Now the underlying securities themselves are priced in the cash market so that they are expected to earn a fair rate of return above the riskless rate to compensate for their risk. This means the return on the futures component of the hedge must just offset the difference between the market return expected on the cash securities and the riskless rate.

For example, suppose that for long-term Treasury bonds the appropriate risk premium over the riskless rate is 2 percent annually. That is, long-term bonds are priced in the market to yield an expected 2 percent more than riskless securities to compensate the investor for the risk of price fluctuation. Eliminating the risk on the deliverable long-term bond by hedging it in the futures market should therefore bring the total expected return down 2 percent to the riskless rate. The futures contract should be priced so that the expected price change as a fraction of the (adjusted) cash price of the deliverable bond is an increase of 2 percent annually. A numerical example will make this clear.

Example: If the cheapest deliverable bond is the 7⅝ of 2007, selling at 71²⁵⁄₃₂, the futures price for delivery thirty-nine days hence should be 74.13, as we calculated above. Assume this bond is priced in the market so that it has an expected annualized return of 10 percent (the repo rate plus 2 percent) over the next thirty-nine days.

In order for it to yield 10 percent, it must satisfy

$$\frac{P_T + A_T}{P + A} = 1 + (0.10)(39/365),$$

where P_T and A_T are price and accrued interest as of the futures expiration date. Solving for P_T gives

$$P_T = (1.0107)(P+A) - A_T$$
$$= (1.0107)(71.78 + 1.96) - 7.625(133/365)$$
$$= 71.75.$$

This implies a futures price at expiration of $71.75/0.9660 = 74.27$. The futures price is therefore expected to rise by $74.27 - 73.78$, for an expected loss on the short sale of 0.49.

Another way of describing the reasoning behind the last argument is to say that, in equilibrium, an investment in any risky security should earn an expected rate of return equal to the current return on riskless securities plus a suitable (market-determined) risk premium. Hedging the security by selling futures transfers the risk from the owner of the security to the buyer of the futures contract. Since he is now bearing the risk, he should earn the risk premium, and the holder of the hedged position should earn the riskless interest rate. The expected return to holding a long futures contract should therefore be the market risk premium on the underlying security of the futures contract. In this case, we have assumed that to be 2 percent annually, or 0.21 percent over the life of the futures contract. The theoretical futures price should therefore be expected to rise by about 0.21 percent to 74.27. Notice that the actual futures price is expected to rise more, since it was initially underpriced relative to the theoretical value. The expected cost of short hedging is higher by the amount of this mispricing.

Unfortunately, there is no real way to know what risk premium the market is assigning to a given security at any point in time, so that this insight into futures price determination does not lead to a precise number for the expected return on a futures contract. However, the order of magnitude can be estimated from past observations on the difference between returns of risky and riskless securities.

The Behavior of the Basis

The return on a partially hedged portfolio will naturally involve the expected return on the cash securities, the expected change in the futures price, and the hedge ratio. The formula can be expressed in terms of the basis – that is, the futures price minus the (adjusted) spot price.

$$R_H = (P_T - P_0) - h(F_T - F_0)$$
$$= (1-h)(P_T - P_0) - h[(F_T - P_T) - (F_0 - P_0)]$$
$$R_H = (1-h)(P_T - P_0) - h(B_T - B_0), \qquad (3.11)$$

where B_0 and B_T refer to the values of the basis at the initial and terminal date of the hedge, time 0 and time T.

This expression makes clear how the return on a hedged position depends on the change in the basis. It says that the total return per unit of the cash security is equal to the return on the portion of the position that is not hedged $(1 - h)$ plus the change in the basis times the fraction that is hedged, h. It is not surprising that hedging has often been characterized as replacing the price risk with potentially more manageable basis risk. Understanding the basis and its dynamics are essential in designing and implementing hedging strategies.

From the outset we can distinguish basis movements that are predictable and should be incorporated into the expected return on a hedged position from those which are unpredictable and which constitute basis risk. Among the former are convergence of the basis toward its theoretical value at times when the cost of carry relation is not satisfied, and convergence to zero at expiration as the futures price becomes equal to the cash price for the cheapest deliverable security. Causes of unpredictable basis movement include changes in the cost of carry, changes in cash market price relationships in the case of a cross hedge, and "noise" arising from imbalances between supply and demand in the futures or the cash market.

The cost of carry model gives the equilibrium price for the futures contract, but because of transactions costs and other frictions in the market, the price can stray away from its theoretical level. Arbitrage forces in the market will then act to bring the price into alignment. How long this process can take and how big a deviation can develop depend on a number of factors. Particularly important is the cost and difficulty of doing the arbitrage trade that is called for. Deviations in the Treasury securities futures contracts tend to be small and transitory, while the stock index contracts appear to exhibit mispricing that is persistent and, at times, quite large (excess returns to the arbitrage trade on the order of 8 percent or more annualized have occurred and have persisted for substantial periods of time). A short hedge when futures are overpriced or a long hedge with underpriced futures can earn an attractive excess return if the position can be held until the equilibrium price relationship is restored.

An important determinant of the behavior of the basis is the amount of time until delivery. From the earlier discussion we know that the shorter the time until delivery, the smaller the total cost of carry will be and, therefore, the narrower the basis will become. At delivery date the basis between futures and the price of the deliverable instrument (adjusted for the delivery factor) should be zero, because the cash and future are effectively interchangeable. This narrowing of the basis over time for the cheapest to deliver security is what we have referred to already as convergence.

Perfect convergence need not occur for every deliverable instrument, only for the cash instrument that is cheapest to deliver (and therefore most likely to be delivered). For any other deliverable or nondeliverable security, the basis will converge to the cash market price differential between it and the adjusted price of the cheapest to deliver cash security. In most cases, this is fairly predictable, although some uncertainty is unavoidable.

The speed of convergence in the futures price can influence the choice of contract month for a hedge if futures are mispriced. When the futures price is below its cost of carry value, long hedges (short the cash position and long the futures contract) will be preferred and nearby month contracts can be chosen since convergence is rapid in the near-delivery months. Similarly, if the future is overpriced, short hedges will be favored, preferably using nearby months. In contrast, if it is necessary to put on long hedges when futures are too high or short hedges when futures are too low, it may be of value to use more distant contract months to try to minimize the effect of convergence during the life of the hedge. Since convergence is still likely to have some adverse effect it might also be appropriate to reduce the hedge ratio to compensate for it.

Since basis is the difference between the futures price and the cash price, any factor that changes the cost of carry will affect the basis. For example, in the case of metal futures, the cost of carry increases with rising interest rates, which in turn would cause basis to widen. In the case of interest rate futures, we have seen how the shape of the yield curve determines whether the basis is positive or negative. A change in the term structure of interest rates will cause a change in the magnitude of the basis, and also possibly its direction.

Consider an increase in the risk free rate. That would increase the total cost of carry from the current date to delivery, which would in turn widen the basis. But for any given cost of carry the basis should be narrowing with decreasing time to delivery, other things being equal. The combined effect of these two factors will determine how the basis moves in response to a change in the cost of carry.

When the cash market instrument being hedged is not deliverable against the futures contract, it is termed a cross-hedge. Here, in studying the dynamics of the basis, it is useful to divide it into two components: (1) the difference between the price of the futures contract and the deliverable underlying cash instrument, and (2) the price difference between the underlying cash instrument and the cash instrument being hedged. Estimating the first component and the factors affecting its dynamics have already been discussed. The second component is more difficult to estimate. Historical data on the yield or price spread between the cash instrument being hedged and the underlying cash instrument are often used to gauge the normal size of this component. Correlation is also used extensively to measure its variability.

Three important factors that are responsible for basis variation in a cross-hedging context are (1) maturity mismatch, (2) differences in liquidity, and (3) differences in credit risk.

Maturity Mismatch.   In many situations the underlying instrument for the futures contract has a maturity different from that of the cash instrument being hedged. For example, an insurance company might use a T-bond futures contract to hedge a portfolio of Treasury bonds of average maturity twelve years. Changes in the shape of the yield curve will cause relative price shifts between twelve-year bonds and the cheapest deliverable issue, which will be reflected in hedge performance. To the extent that such term structure changes are predictable (and the hedger wishes to speculate on the accuracy of his predictions), an adjustment to the hedge ratio might be worthwhile. The hedge will be reduced when an unfavorable basis shift is anticipated and increased when a favorable change is expected.

Differences in Liquidity.   If the cash instrument being hedged is not traded in a liquid market, its price can fluctuate relatively far when large transactions are made. This will lead to transitory changes in the basis. The more liquid the market for the cash instrument, the less basis variation one would expect.

Differences in Credit Risk.   Often the credit risk of the cash instrument being hedged is different from that of the cash instrument underlying the futures contract. An example would be when T-bond futures are used to hedge a portfolio of corporate bonds.

The normal yield differentials for different segments of the debt market can be estimated from historical data, but deviations from "customary" relationships can be substantial in the case of very dissimilar instruments and can persist for long periods relative to the holding period of many hedges. A good example is the relationship between Treasury and tax-exempt yields, which has varied widely in the past several years. Again, to the extent that a change in yield differential can be predicted, the hedge can be tailored to take advantage of it (or minimize its adverse impact) and increase returns. To the extent that yield shifts cannot be predicted, they become another source of basis risk and should be countered by reducing the hedge ratio.

Still another reason for the basis to change is the possibility that over the hedging period a different bond will become the cheapest to deliver, either because of realignment in market yields or because of a new issue by the Treasury. In contrast to the other factors we have been discussing, having a new bond take the place of cheapest delivery usually has a one-sided effect on a hedge: The futures price will drop relative to the cost of carry level based on the previously cheapest bond, because the deliverable quantity of the new bond costs less. This means that a long position in the formerly cheapest bond hedged by short futures contracts will experience an extra return. On the other hand, if the new bond has significantly different coupon or maturity from the old one, cross-hedge correlation will be affected and an adjustment to the hedge may be called for.

If the credit rating of the cash instrument is not as high as the underlying deliverable cash instrument, the correlation in price movement will be reduced and variation in the basis will increase. Correlation analysis will identify the best futures contract to use for hedging. An adjustment to the basis computation can be made by determining from historical price spreads the price difference between the deliverable instrument and the hedged cash instrument.

Lastly, there is the catchall category of explanation called "noise." The basis fluctuates randomly from minute to minute during the trading day and from one day to the next for reasons that are not always understood. The source of these changes in the basis may be altered expectations among the market population, imbalances in supply and demand in the futures market or the cash market, and a myriad of other things. These changes introduce basis risk into any hedge, but the effect is attenuated for longer duration hedges. A hedged position held for only a day or two can be subject to considerable basis risk from such unexplained factors, but basis risk from "noise" in one held for a month or more will become a fairly small component of total risk, and therefore less important a problem. In certain cases in which the hedger has flexibility in choosing when to put on and lift the hedge, basis fluctuations from transitory causes may provide the opportunity to increase returns by timing the hedge trades so that they are done when the basis is favorable.

4 HEDGING WITH TREASURY BOND FUTURES IN PRACTICE

The last two chapters have described how a futures hedge works and how to analyze a given hedging situation in order to determine the appropriate way to set up a hedge. In this chapter we will examine two cases in detail. Both involve the use of Treasury bond futures to reduce the vulnerability of a cash position in bonds to interest rate fluctuations. We illustrate the procedure for analyzing and structuring a hedge using actual market data from June 1982 through December 1983, and then examine the performance of the hedge during the first ten months of 1984.

The first example is a hedge of a portfolio of four Treasury bonds of varying maturity. Because of the similarity between the cash portfolio and the deliverable instrument for the bond futures contract, a very good hedge is possible. The second case is a little trickier. We look at hedging an investment in a single corporate issue, the Alcoa 13⅛ of 2011, which is rated A by Standard and Poor's. Here, since the cash instrument is a corporate bond and is also a single issue rather than a diversified portfolio, the hedge will tend to be less effective. However, a significant risk reduction is still possible if the effect of basis risk is correctly taken into account in computing the hedge ratio. We then illustrate the impact of basis risk on the choice of the hedge ratio. In both cases, failure to adjust for basis risk leads to overhedging and reduced hedge effectiveness.

We end the chapter with an example in which the price in the futures market is used in setting the rate on a GIC commitment, that is then hedged with T-bond futures.

EXAMPLE 1: HEDGING A PORTFOLIO OF TREASURY BONDS

The cash position to be hedged consists of a portfolio containing $5 million face value of each of the following four Treasury bonds.

13¾ of May 1992
10⅜ of May 1995
11¾ of February 2001
14 of November 2011

These bonds were chosen for this example because they have each been outstanding for long enough that a history of past price changes is available, yet they are not so seasoned that they no longer trade in a liquid market. The average maturity of the portfolio at the beginning of 1984 was about sixteen years, just over the minimum maturity for a bond to be deliverable against the futures contract. Of course, this portfolio could not actually be delivered, since only the two longest bonds fit the criteria. Still, the portfolio's yield movements should follow closely those of other bonds in the maturity range tracked by the futures contract.

The hedging period starts at the beginning of 1984. We will consider ten consecutive one-month holding periods ending in October 1984 and assume that the objective of the hedge is to minimize the standard deviation of month-to-month changes in the total return on the portfolio. That is, we will be trying to create a risk minimizing hedged position during the ten-month period. In order to do this, we will begin by analyzing price changes on the individual bonds and the portfolio as a whole during the eighteen months prior, from July 1982 through December 1983, and relating them to the price movements in the Treasury bond futures contracts over that period.

Table 4–1 shows month ending prices for the four bonds during the entire period under consideration, June 1982 to October 1984. The portfolio consisting of $5 million face value of each had the total value shown in the fifth column of the table. Dividing by the combined face value of $20 million gives what might be considered the "price" of the portfolio on the basis of par equals 100. The final column then shows the series of monthly portfolio price changes. In addition to the price change, the cash portfolio accrues coupon interest of $207,813 per month. This implies an effective coupon rate of 1.039 percent monthly or 12.47 annually for the portfolio.

Table 4-1.   Prices of Treasury Bonds in Hedged Portfolio 6/82–10/84.

Month	13¾ of 1992	10⅜ of 1995	11¾ of 2001	14s of 2011	Portfolio value	Portfolio price	Portfolio price change
82 06	96.50	78.06	84.97	100.56	18,004,660	90.02	—
82 07	100.38	81.69	88.22	104.19	18,723,410	93.62	3.59
82 08	105.19	87.00	94.50	111.66	19,917,150	99.59	5.97
82 09	111.13	93.13	100.78	119.00	21,201,550	106.01	6.42
82 10	115.19	98.09	106.97	125.88	22,306,235	111.53	5.52
82 11	114.25	97.19	105.50	123.69	22,031,225	110.16	−1.38
82 12	116.41	99.00	107.53	126.69	22,481,200	112.41	2.25
83 01	113.97	96.38	103.31	120.75	21,720,300	108.60	−3.80
83 02	117.66	100.16	107.63	126.66	22,604,650	113.02	4.42
83 03	115.81	98.31	105.84	125.03	22,249,975	111.25	−1.77
83 04	117.94	100.44	108.81	128.88	22,803,050	114.02	2.77
83 05	114.94	96.69	104.25	122.25	21,906,225	109.53	−4.48
83 06	113.63	95.63	103.41	122.41	21,753,100	108.77	−0.77
83 07	109.00	90.81	98.50	115.13	20,671,875	103.36	−5.41
83 08	108.25	90.44	97.09	114.28	20,503,110	102.52	−0.84
83 09	111.13	93.13	100.78	119.00	21,201,550	106.01	3.49
83 10	109.94	91.69	98.84	116.25	20,835,910	104.18	−1.83
83 11	110.66	92.41	99.91	118.41	21,068,720	105.34	1.16
83 12	109.59	91.28	98.59	116.81	20,814,045	104.07	−1.27
84 01	110.44	92.41	100.13	117.81	21,039,010	105.20	1.12
84 02	108.63	89.94	97.34	114.19	20,504,660	102.52	−2.67
84 03	105.81	87.47	94.41	110.75	19,921,845	99.61	−2.91
84 04	104.19	85.81	92.13	108.28	19,520,275	97.60	−2.01
84 05	99.28	80.44	86.13	101.28	18,356,235	91.78	−5.82
84 06	99.44	80.63	86.56	102.06	18,434,350	92.17	0.39
84 07	103.59	85.28	91.91	108.13	19,445,320	97.23	5.05
84 08	104.03	86.00	93.44	109.69	19,657,775	98.29	1.06
84 09	105.75	87.97	95.44	113.88	20,151,560	100.76	2.47
84 10	109.63	92.06	99.88	118.22	20,989,075	104.95	4.19

In Table 4–2 we show the futures price changes for the same period. In all cases we are looking at the futures contract closest to expiration, which is the one with the highest liquidity. Since the two examples in this chapter both involve a one-month hedging horizon, the nearest contract (with more than one month to expiration) is the most appropriate to use in the hedge. If we were considering long holding periods,

Table 4–2. Price Changes for Treasury Bond Futures Contract Nearest to Expiration.

Month	Price change	Contract month
82 07	2.13	SEP 82
82 08	4.19	SEP 82
82 09	4.38	DEC 82
82 10	5.47	DEC 82
82 11	−1.13	DEC 82
82 12	1.78	MAR 83
83 01	−3.31	MAR 83
83 02	3.97	MAR 83
83 03	−0.72	JUN 83
83 04	2.97	JUN 83
83 05	−4.28	JUN 83
83 06	0.31	SEP 83
83 07	−4.44	SEP 83
83 08	−0.16	SEP 83
83 09	3.50	DEC 83
83 10	−2.03	DEC 83
83 11	0.94	DEC 83
83 12	−1.03	MAR 84
84 01	0.78	MAR 84
84 02	−1.97	MAR 84
84 03	−2.00	JUN 84
84 04	−1.53	JUN 84
84 05	−4.53	JUN 84
84 06	0.16	SEP 84
84 07	4.88	SEP 84
84 08	1.31	SEP 84
84 09	2.06	DEC 84
84 10	3.56	DEC 84

it might be better to pick a more distant contract in order to avoid having to roll over the futures as the nearest contracts expired, but in this case the hedge maturity matches the shortest contract.

As of the beginning of January 1984, we would have had available only the data in the first parts of Tables 4-1 and 4-2, relating to price changes up to that time. In order to determine the risk-minimizing hedge ratio, we run the regression of price changes of the cash position regressed on futures price changes over the same period. With eighteen observations, that regression yields

$$DC = -0.04 + 1.18 \ DF \qquad R^2 = 0.96$$
$$\quad (0.033) \quad (0.004) \qquad SER = 0.75$$
$$\text{Sample: } 7/82 - 12/83. \qquad (4.1)$$

The very high R^2 indicates that the futures contract tracked the value of the portfolio extremely well during this period. If this relationship continued, a good hedge should be quite possible for 1984. The standard error of regression was 0.75, meaning that the value of an optimally hedged position during the sample period would have experienced a monthly standard deviation of only 0.75, or around three-quarters of a percent, versus about 3.68 percent for the portfolio held unhedged.

Since there are data available on the daily prices of all of these bonds, would there have been any value to running the regression on a larger number of data points by taking more frequent observations? Aside from the increased burden in computation from dealing with more data, one reason to prefer monthly data for estimation is that the effect of basis risk on a hedge varies with the length of the holding period. If we had used daily data in the regression (4.1), the basis movement would have been a larger component of the total futures price change than it is for monthly data. The regression would not have fit as well (lower R^2), and the regression coefficient would have been smaller. To obtain reliable estimates of the future h^* and of hedging effectiveness, the differencing interval used in the estimation of hedge parameters should not be too short unless the hedge is only going to be held for a short period also. By the same token, a hedge that is only going to be in place for a week, or a day, is exposed to substantially more basis risk than is one to be held for a month. In that case, use of weekly or daily data is called for to take full account of the basis risk in the estimation.

From equation (2.13) in Chapter 2, the number of futures contracts to use in the hedge is equal to h^* multiplied by the face value of the cash position and divided by the face value of a futures contract. In this case, that gives

Number of Futures Contracts $= (1.18) \times (20,000,000)/(100,000)$
$$= 236.$$

The minimum risk hedge involves selling 236 Treasury bond futures contracts against the long position in $20 million of government bonds.

Table 4-3 shows the results of that strategy during 1984. It can be seen that the first ten months of 1984 were a fairly turbulent period for the bond market. In two months the market value of the portfolio changed by more than 5 percent, and in half of the months a swing of over $500,000 was recorded. Although, in the end, the mean change in value was only $17,503, the risk was great; standard deviation was nearly $650,000. While an investor with a longer holding period would have experienced these fluctuations in value as transitory, the risk was very real for anyone making transactions during this period because they would have had to trade at widely varying prices.

Including accrued interest, the returns on the portfolio held un-hedged averaged 1.19 per month with a standard deviation of 3.52 percent. The total return over the whole period was 10.83 percent.

The short futures position lost on average $64,166 per month with a standard deviation of about $640,000. Comparing the cash flows on the futures hedge with the changes in market value for the bond portfolio, it is clear that they match rather well. The total hedged return averaged $161,149 per month, and the effectiveness of the hedge is apparent in the fact that standard deviation went down by a factor of over ten. A mark of the success of the hedge is that in no month did the hedged portfolio experience a loss.

The risk-minimizing hedge ratio from the regression, h^*, was 1.18. Let us look at the result of running the regression on the price changes that occurred during our hedging period in 1984 to see how close the estimate of h^* from historical data was to the true minimum risk hedge ratio.

$$DC = -0.11 \quad + 1.19 \quad DF \qquad R^2 = 0.99$$
$$(0.012) \quad (0.002) \qquad SER = 0.35$$
$$\text{Sample: } 1/84 - 10/84. \qquad (4.2)$$

In this case, the results are extraordinarily close. The estimate of h^* is virtually identical, and the regression fits even better than it did for

Table 4-3. Results of Hedge of Treasury Bond Portfolio during 1984. 236 Contracts Sold ($h = 1.18$).

Month	Change in market value	Coupon interest	Total return unhedged	% Return unhedged	Profit on futures hedge	Total hedged return	% Return on hedge
JAN 84	224,965	207,813	432,778	2.08	-184,387	248,391	1.19
FEB	-534,350	207,813	-326,537	-1.55	464,637	138,099	0.66
MAR	-582,815	207,813	-375,002	-1.83	472,000	96,998	0.47
APR	-401,570	207,813	-193,757	-0.97	361,363	167,606	0.84
MAY	-1,164,040	207,813	-956,227	-4.90	1,069,363	113,136	0.58
JUN	78,115	207,813	285,928	1.56	-36,887	249,041	1.36
JUL	1,010,970	207,813	1,218,783	6.61	-1,150,500	68,282	0.37
AUG	212,455	207,813	420,268	2.16	-309,750	110,518	0.57
SEPT	493,785	207,813	701,598	3.57	-486,750	214,848	1.09
OCT	837,515	207,813	1,045,328	5.19	-840,750	204,578	1.02
Mean	17,503	207,813	225,316	1.19	-64,166	161,149	0.81
Standard deviation	648,656	0	648,656	3.52	637,994	61,877	0.32
10-month total	175,030	2,078,125	2,253,160	10.83	-641,660	1,611,495	7.74

the sample period. R^2 is up over 0.99, and the standard error of regression has been reduced substantially. It must be said that such similarity between coefficient estimates from two different sample periods is unusual. This should not necessarily be taken as representative of what will be experienced in normal hedging operations.

Hedging with Treasury bond futures was extremely successful in reducing risk on this portfolio. What was the cost of doing so? Mean monthly returns went down from 1.19 percent to 0.81 percent, which translated to a drop in total return over the whole period from 10.83 percent to 7.74 percent. The overall result is as it should be: the hedge reduced risk at the cost of diminished return. The cost of insurance in this case was about 3 percent over ten months.

EXAMPLE 2: HEDGING A CORPORATE BOND

Next we will turn to an example which has more of the elements of a cross-hedge than the previous one. That is, the cash position being hedged is different in character from the underlying securities for the futures contract. Assume that at the beginning of 1984, the object was to minimize the risk of price fluctuation on a holding of $5 million face value of the Alcoa Aluminum 13 ⅞ of 2011 bonds. This is a corporate issue, and as such it will behave somewhat differently from the Treasury bonds underlying the T-bond futures contract. It has a twenty-seven-year maturity, which is longer than the bonds that would normally be delivered against futures, and it is exposed to price fluctuation due to credit risk. The latter may be significant, as the bond is rated A by Standard and Poor's. Price variability associated with changes in the market's perception of the risk of default or impairment of debt coverage on a corporate bond cannot be hedged by a futures contract based on default-free Treasury issues. Moreover, since we are dealing with the securities of a single issuer, portfolio diversification that reduces the effects of transitory market imbalances in a particular bond does not help here.

As before, monthly data on the bond's price movements were obtained for the period from July 1982 through October 1984. These are shown in Table 4–4. The concurrent price change for the relevant T-bond futures contract is also displayed. Casual inspection gives the impression that while the two price change series are similar, there are months like August 1982 in which they exhibit considerable independence of movement.

Equation (4.3) gives the results of the regression of the price change

Table 4-4.   Prices of Alcoa 13⅞s of 2011. 6/82–10/84.

Month	Bond price	Bond price change	Futures price change
82 06	85.00	—	—
82 07	87.13	2.13	2.13
82 08	97.50	10.38	4.19
82 09	99.00	1.50	4.38
82 10	100.75	1.75	5.47
82 11	105.75	5.00	−1.13
82 12	103.44	−2.31	1.78
83 01	105.34	1.91	−3.31
83 02	108.91	3.56	3.97
83 03	108.91	0.00	−0.72
83 04	111.41	2.50	2.97
83 05	107.69	−3.72	−4.28
83 06	106.91	−0.78	0.31
83 07	100.50	−6.41	−4.44
83 08	101.19	0.69	−0.16
83 09	104.53	3.34	3.50
83 10	102.63	−1.91	−2.03
83 11	103.03	0.41	0.94
83 12	104.16	1.13	−1.03
84 01	104.94	0.78	0.78
84 02	103.03	−1.91	−1.97
84 03	101.50	−1.53	−2.00
84 04	98.38	−3.13	−1.53
84 05	93.53	−4.84	−4.53
84 06	94.19	0.66	0.16
84 07	98.44	4.25	4.88
84 08	99.78	1.34	1.31
84 09	101.91	2.12	2.06
84 10	101.50	−0.41	3.56

of the bond on the futures price change over the eighteen-month sampling period.

$$DC = -0.56 + 0.72 \ DF \qquad R^2 = 0.37$$
$$ (0.51) \quad (0.055) \qquad SER = 2.95$$
$$\text{Sample: } 7/82 - 12/83. \qquad (4.3)$$

The R^2 of this regression confirms the impression that the future does not track the value of this bond as well as it did the portfolio of Treasuries we looked at above. The correlation coefficient between the two series is only 0.61. Still, if the linear relationship that has been fitted here continues to hold during the hedging period, some risk reduction is possible.

Using $h^* = 0.72$, the number of bond futures contracts to sell was

$$\text{Number of Futures Contracts} = 0.72 \times \frac{5,000,000}{100,000}$$

$$= 36 \text{ contracts.}$$

Table 4–5 gives the monthly returns on the position. During the early part of the year, the bond experienced substantial losses in value, followed by a price recovery during the summer. Overall, it lost value in five out of ten months. Adding in the monthly accrued interest of $57,813 still left losses in four months. The mean return was 0.94 percent per month, with a standard deviation of 2.74.

Turning to the returns on the futures hedge, we see that in nine out of ten months, the hedge served to offset a portion of the change in value of the bond position. Although the magnitudes were not equal, the net effect was to smooth out the market fluctuations. Only in October did the hedge really backfire, with a substantial loss on futures exacerbating a small loss on the cash bonds. Comparing the risk and return on the hedged versus the unhedged position, hedging reduced the standard deviation by about half, at a cost of 0.23 percent per month, or 1.88 percent over the ten months.

If we run the regression on the price changes that were experienced during 1984, we get

$$DC = -0.49 + 0.83 \quad DF \qquad\qquad R^2 = 0.78$$
$$(0.18) \quad (0.024) \qquad\qquad SER = 1.33$$
$$\text{Sample: } 1/84 - 10/84. \qquad (4.4)$$

The regression coefficient, though not identical to the one estimated from the earlier data, is actually fairly close, given the relatively low explanatory power of that equation. An interesting change is that the R^2 of the equation has increased markedly, which means that the hedge was more effective in 1984 than in the sample period. The correlation coefficient went up to 0.88, and the standard deviation of the price change on the bond dropped from 3.51 to 2.53.

Table 4-5. Monthly Returns on Alcoa Bond Position during 1984. 36 Contracts Sold ($h = 0.72$).

Month	Change in market value	Coupon interest	Total return unhedged	% Return unhedged	Profit on futures hedge	Total hedged return	% Return on hedge
JAN 84	39,050	57,813	96,862	1.86	−28,127	68,736	1.32
FEB	−95,300	57,813	−37,487	−0.71	70,877	33,389	0.64
MAR	−76,550	57,813	−18,738	−0.36	72,000	53,262	1.03
APR	−156,250	57,813	−98,438	−1.94	55,123	−43,314	−0.85
MAY	−242,190	57,813	−184,378	−3.75	163,123	−21,254	−0.43
JUN	32,815	57,813	90,628	1.94	−5,627	85,001	1.82
JUL	217,500	57,813	270,313	5.74	−175,500	94,813	2.01
AUG	67,185	57,813	124,997	2.54	−47,250	77,747	1.58
SEPT	106,240	57,813	164,053	3.29	−74,250	89,803	1.80
OCT	−20,300	57,813	37,512	0.74	−128,250	−90,738	−1.78
Mean	−13,280	57,813	44,533	0.94	−9,788	34,744	0.71
Standard deviation	126,578	—	126,578	2.74	102,585	64,541	1.30
10-month total	−132,800	578,125	445,325	8.55	−97,880	347,445	6.67

Thus, in this case we see the effect of basis risk in the cross-hedge. Although the hedge ratio we used was fairly close to the risk-minimizing value, only about half of the risk was eliminated, and there was one month in which the hedger was clearly worse off than if he had not used futures at all. Still, the opportunity to reduce the standard deviation of the monthly return from 2.74 percent to 1.30 percent may well have been of considerable value, even though a perfect hedge was impossible.

THE EFFECTS OF OVERHEDGING

An important reason to estimate hedge ratios from the price change regression, as we have done, is that basis risk is taken into account automatically. Other approaches either adjust only approximately or, worse, ignore it altogether. Ignoring the effect of basis risk in setting up a hedge will normally lead to overhedging—the hedge ratio will be too high because no account is taken of the fact that while trading futures against a cash position offsets risk due to interest rate changes, it adds risk from fluctuations in the basis.

Suppose that instead of estimating h^* by regression in our examples, we had simply computed the conversion factors for the bonds as if they were deliverable against the futures contracts and used those as hedge ratios. This is a procedure that is often recommended for setting hedge ratios.

The conversion factor, as discussed above, is the price the bond in question would have in order to yield 8 percent, divided by 100. This is easily computed by taking the present value of the coupons to be paid and the face value at maturity, discounted at 8 percent. For example, to yield 8 percent to maturity, the Treasury 14s of 2011 as of the beginning of 1984 would have been priced at 166.66. The conversion factor for them was therefore 1.6666. If this had been used as the hedge ratio, the ratio of futures contracts to cash bonds would have been five to three (i.e., five futures contracts sold for every $300,000 of face value of bonds held). In this case, hedging $5 million face value of these bonds would have required selling eighty-three T-bond contracts.

The conversion factors for the four bonds in the portfolio were as follows:

13¾ of 1992	1.3498
10⅜ of 1995	1.1764
11¾ of 2001	1.3452
14 of 2011	1.6666

The (weighted) average factor for the whole portfolio is 1.3845. If a hedge ratio of 1.38 had been used in the hedge, 276 futures contracts would have been sold against the portfolio, instead of the 236 that we looked at before.

Table 4–6 compares the results of the two different hedge proportions. The first two lines duplicate the figures from Table 4–3, showing the performance of the risk-minimizing hedge. When a larger futures position is taken, one can see that hedging effectiveness has decreased. The monthly standard deviation of the return nearly doubles, from 0.32 percent to 0.61 percent, and at the same time the mean return drops by 0.06 percent. That is the normal result of overhedging: The more futures that are sold, the lower expected return becomes, while once the risk-minimizing h^* is passed, the standard deviation begins to rise.

The cost of overhedging here is not actually too bad. The standard deviation doubled but from such a low level that the hedge still achieved considerable risk reduction. Unhedged, the standard deviation on this portfolio was 3.52 percent monthly. The loss in return was only about one half of one percent over the ten-month period. The reason is that basis risk in this hedge was not very large, so that ignoring it did not change the hedge ratio by that much.

The situation is significantly different for the hedge of the Alcoa 13⅞ bonds. Because of its high coupon and long maturity, this bond had a large conversion factor of 1.6527. Using this as a hedge ratio would have led to selling eighty-three bond futures contracts against the $5 million cash position. Since the minimum risk hedge was to sell thirty-six contracts, the amount of overhedging was considerable. The second part of Table 4–6 shows the consequences on hedge performance. Again the standard deviation of return on the hedged position approximately doubled, but this time it was from a higher value than for the previous example. The result was that the standard deviation on the "hedge" was virtually the same as on the bond portfolio with no hedge. At the same time, selling such a large number of futures reduced returns from 0.94 percent per month to 0.43 percent, a difference

Table 4-6. Hedge Performance with No Adjustment for Basis Risk.

Portfolio	Number of futures contracts	Mean return	Standard deviation	Maximum	Minimum	10-month total
Treasury issues	236	$161,149 0.81%	$61,877 0.32%	$249,041 1.36%	$−68,282 −0.37%	$1,611,495 7.74%
Treasury issues	276	$150,274 0.75%	$117,667 0.61%	$294,384 1.51%	$−126,717 −0.69%	$1,502,744 7.22%
Alcoa 13⅞ of 2011	36	$34,744 0.71%	$64,541 1.30%	$94,813 2.01%	$−90,378 −1.78%	$347,445 6.67%
Alcoa 13⅞ of 2011	83	$21,966 0.43%	$127,417 2.54%	$191,712 3.90%	$−258,175 −5.07%	$219,656 4.22%

of 4.33 percent over the entire ten months. Moreover, the highest monthly return on this position was lower than for the portfolio held unhedged, while the biggest monthly loss was worse. Ignoring the impact of basis risk in estimating the correct hedge proportion would have been a serious mistake.

The overall message of this section is this. Because there is a trade-off between risk and return in the marketplace, bearing the risk of price fluctuation on an investment in bonds (or any other security) is normally rewarded with higher expected return. Hedging risk away in the futures market reduces expected return. The cost in terms of performance for underhedging is not severe: More risk is borne, but expected returns are greater. By contrast, the cost of overhedging is much more serious. Once the minimum risk hedge ratio is passed, expected return continues to go down, but risk begins to rise. The over-hedged position is worse than the correctly hedged position on both counts. It has lower expected return *and* higher risk. As a consequence, a prudent hedger should regard the risk-minimizing hedge ratio that he estimates by whatever method not as the hedge ratio that he should use but rather as the *maximum* hedge ratio that could be considered. To the extent that basis risk and estimation error lend uncertainty to the calculation of h^*, the hedge ratio should be reduced, to avoid the risk that the position will end up being overhedged.

HEDGING THE YIELD SPREAD ON A GIC COMMITMENT

One of the important uses of futures markets is in pricing cash market transactions. In fact, part of the examination undertaken by the Commodity Futures Trading Commission in deciding on whether to permit trading in a proposed new futures contract concerns whether it would contribute to "price discovery." That is, would prices generated in the futures market contain valuable information that could be used by cash market participants, independent of whether they trade futures? In agricultural commodities, for example, it is common for dealers and producers to base storage and production decisions on the level of prices in the futures market and then to hedge the decisions that are made with futures. Financial futures offer the same type of opportunities to financial institutions.

For example, life insurance companies are heavily involved in writing guaranteed interest contracts (GICs) that are purchased, typically, by pension funds and other long-term investors. The GIC guarantees an interest rate on invested funds over a period of a number of years, and the market for GICs has become so competitive that in order to meet the contractual payments, an insurance company must invest the proceeds in high yielding securities and manage the funds carefully. Frequently, GICs carry an added dimension of risk in the fact that there is a commitment period during which the insurance company has fixed the rate it will offer but the funds have not yet been transferred. If interest rates in the market should drop during the commitment period, the company may find that it can not invest the proceeds of the GIC at a high enough yield to cover its costs. Or it might be lucky and see rates rise during the commitment period, leading to an unanticipated extra profit. In any case, fixing its borrowing rate before having the funds available to invest exposes the issuer of the GIC to interest rate risk.

In this section we will discuss an example in which prices in the Treasury bond futures market are used first to determine the rate that will be offered on a GIC commitment, and then bond futures are used to hedge that rate over the commitment period.

What is an appropriate rate to pay on a GIC? One way to approach the problem is to offer a rate based on the yields currently available on Treasury securities. Let us consider the case of an issuer whose policy is to base the rate offered on GICs on the yield implied by prices in the Treasury bond futures market. Assume that the GIC rate is set always twenty-five basis points above the yield for the 8 percent reference bond, and suppose that in order to cover the liability the proceeds are to be invested in the Alcoa 13 ⅞ of 2011 bonds we have been examining above. Over the period from June 1982 through December 1983, the mean end-of-month spread between these two yields, less twenty-five basis points, was 1.30 percent, with a standard deviation of 0.45, which the issuer believes will provide an adequate return on the transaction.

The contracts will be offered with a one-month commitment period, during which the promised rate will be hedged in the Treasury bond futures market. In this case, the concern is that yields will go down during the period and it will not be possible to invest the proceeds of the GIC profitably when they become available. Thus the appropriate hedge is a long hedge, buying T-bond futures that will rise in price if yields drop.

The hedge is just the opposite of what we looked at before—that is, thirty-six Treasury bond futures contracts will be purchased. At the end of the commitment period, any profit or loss will be added to the $5 million cash inflow and the total will be invested. One way to think about the effect of this hedging transaction is that it changes the effective price (and yield) on the bonds that are purchased. For example, if the bonds are selling at par at the end of the period and $50,000 has been made on the futures hedge, the effective bond price becomes $100 \times (5,000,000/5,050,000) = 99.00$, since one has essentially used $5 million to buy a larger quantity of bonds.

Let us examine the performance of this strategy over the first ten months of 1984.

Table 4–7 shows the results by month. The first column gives the yield that was set on the GIC, which was twenty-five basis points above the yield to maturity on the 8 percent twenty-year reference bond im-

Table 4–7.   Yield Spread on Hedged GIC Commitment.

Month	Yield committed on GIC	Actual investment yield	Profit on futures hedge	Effective bond price	Effective investment yield
JAN 84	12.23	13.20	28,127	104.35	13.27
FEB	12.09	13.45	−70,877	104.51	13.25
MAR	12.44	13.65	−72,000	102.98	13.45
APR	12.93	14.10	−55,123	99.47	13.93
MAY	13.24	14.85	−163,123	96.69	14.35
JUN	14.21	14.75	5,627	94.08	14.77
JUL	14.34	14.10	175,500	95.10	14.60
AUG	13.28	13.90	47,250	98.85	14.03
SEP	13.02	13.60	74,250	100.42	13.80
OCT	12.74	13.66	128,250	98.96	14.01

	Unhedged	Hedged
Mean yield spread	0.87	0.89
Standard deviation	0.53	0.31
Highest	1.61	1.26
Lowest	−0.24	0.26

plied by the futures price as of the last trading day of the previous month. The second column shows the actual yield that was obtained when the Alcoa bonds were purchased one month later. The futures hedge returns are just the negative of those shown in Table 4-5 for the same months. These translated into the effective bond prices and yields displayed in the last two columns.

The important statistics are those shown at the bottom for the mean and standard deviation of the yield spread. Without hedging, the aver-age spread was 0.87 with a standard deviation of 0.53. In one month, this shrank to a spread of −24 basis points, making it a rather unattractive deal. When the promised rate was hedged in the bond futures market, the effective yield actually rose by two basis points at the same time that the standard deviation was dropping considerably. Although there was a fair amount of basis risk in the hedge, as we saw in the previous example, it was effective in moderating the risk of yield movement during the commitment period. In the worst month, the spread was still 0.26.

In this example, we assumed that the GIC issuer was willing to bear the risk of interest rate changes once the funds were invested. However, since the GIC liability was of shorter maturity than the assets held against it, it would still be exposed to risk throughout its life. In the next chapter we will described immunization strategies designed to hedge the risks arising from maturity mismatches such as this.

5 THE USE OF FUTURES IN IMMUNIZATION STRATEGIES

In Chapter 2 we discussed how both a bond's maturity and coupon rate affected its exposure to risk from interest rate fluctuations. This chapter will describe the concept of "duration," which provides a convenient way to summarize this yield sensitivity in a single number, which can then be used in setting up hedge strategies to immunize against interest rate risk.

DURATION DEFINED

Duration is one of the most important concepts for fixed-income risk management. As developed by Macaulay in the 1930s, a fixed-income security's duration is a weighted average term to maturity of its stream of cash flows. The "maturity" of each individual cash flow (the number of periods remaining until it is received) is weighted by the fraction it contributes to the security's total present value. For example, a five-year, 10 percent coupon bond currently priced at $926.40 per $1,000 of par value has a yield to maturity of 12 percent and a duration of 4.01 years (formula to be provided below). This duration of 4.01 years is a more meaningful measure of the bond's "effective" life than its five-year term to maturity, because term to maturity considers only the timing of the bond's final payment while duration also takes into account the size and timing of the bond's coupon payments and their contribution to the bond's total present value. Intuitively, duration measures the life of a series of cash flows in terms of the term to maturity of an "equivalent" zero coupon bond. Thus, the 4.01 year duration of the five-year, 10 percent coupon bond means that this particular bond currently has approximately the same risk as a four-year zero coupon bond.

Duration provides a simple but useful measure of a security's price sensitivity to changes in yield. More specifically, duration is the security's price "elasticity" with respect to a small change in its gross yield, where the term elasticity refers to the percentage price change divided by the percentage change in gross yield (i.e., 1 + the yield to maturity). Duration can therefore be viewed as an index by which to rank alternative fixed-income securities according to their price risk. For any given change in yields, high duration securities are more price volatile (in percentage terms) than low duration securities. This makes duration useful in evaluating interest rate risk. In particular, asset/liability "immunization" strategies designed to eliminate net portfolio risk typically use duration-based techniques.

Futures contracts can be readily incorporated into duration-based immunization strategies, providing the investment officer with important new flexibility in achieving portfolio immunization. This chapter is devoted to providing a brief review of the duration concept and outlining some basic immunization strategies involving the use of futures contracts.

A Duration Formula

The formula to calculate the duration (D) of a security that has just paid a coupon is

$$D = [C_1/P(1+R_1)^1](1) + [C_2/P(1+R_2)^2](2) + \cdots$$

$$+ [(C_T+F)/P(1+R_T)^T](T);$$

$$= \frac{1}{P}\left[\sum_{t=1}^{T} \frac{C_t t}{(1+R_t)^t} + \frac{FT}{(1+R_T)^T} \right], \tag{5.1}$$

where the timing index ($t = 1, 2, \ldots, T$) indicates the number of periods until each individual coupon, C_t, is received; $(1+R_t)$ is the per period discount factor; F is the face value; and P is the security's current price. Since R_t is the discount rate to apply on a single cash flow occurring at date t, for precision, it is best to take R values from the zero coupon yield curve. Thus, a security's duration actually is a function of only three fundamental factors: (1) the amounts in the cash flow series, (2) the timing of those flows, and (3) the current term structure of yields. The fourth factor appearing in the duration equation, P, is implied by the first three through the basic pricing relation:

$$P = C_1/(1+R_1) + C_2/(1+R_2)^2 + \cdots + (C_T+F)/(1+R_T)^T. \qquad (5.2)$$

Equation 5.2 represents a more general form of equation (1.8) that allows for the possibility that the zero coupon yield curve may call for different discount rates for cash flows received at different points in time. A comparison of the duration and present value equations should reinforce the interpretation that duration is a weighted average term to maturity measure where the weights for each period reflect the contribution of its cash flow to total present value.

An Example

For simplicity, assume that a single per period discount factor is applied to all cash flows — that is, the current term structure is flat. It was asserted earlier that a five-year maturity, 10 percent coupon, 12 percent yield bond has a duration of 4.01 years (8.02 semiannual periods). Table 5-1 presents the worksheet used to make this calculation. The five columns in this table present: (1) the "maturity" of each individual cash flow; (2) the amount of each cash flow; (3) the present value of each cash flow (discounted at the bond's yield to maturity, as is appropriate under the flat term structure assumption); (4) the fractional weights applied to each maturity's cash flow; and (5) the individual weighted maturities of each cash flow. The sum of the ten elements of column five is the bond's duration.

While this worksheet may make duration calculation appear somewhat cumbersome, the duration of any security is quite simple to determine with the aid of duration tables or a computer spreadsheet program. Also, when the yield curve is flat, as we are assuming here, a convenient expression for a bond's duration exists. Duration is given by a simple function of R, the bond's yield to maturity; CR ($= C/F$), the bond's coupon rate; τ, the fraction of a year remaining until pay-

Table 5-1. Computing the Duration of a 5-Year, 10% Coupon Bond Priced at $926.40 to Yield 12%.

Cash flow "maturities" (1)	Cash flow amount (2)	Discount factor (3)*	Fractional present value weights (4)**	Weighted cash flow maturities (5)
0.5	50	0.943	0.051	0.026
1.0	50	0.890	0.048	0.048
1.5	50	0.840	0.045	0.068
2.0	50	0.792	0.043	0.086
2.5	50	0.747	0.040	0.100
3.0	50	0.705	0.038	0.114
3.5	50	0.665	0.036	0.126
4.0	50	0.627	0.034	0.136
4.5	50	0.592	0.032	0.144
5.0	1,050	0.558	0.633	3.165

Duration $= 4.01$

*$(1/1.06)^t$, where t is expressed in number of semiannual periods [2 times column (1)].
**Column (2) times column (3) divided by $926.40.

ment of the bond's next coupon (to account correctly for a bond that is currently between interest payments); N, the total number of coupon payments remaining; and m, the number of times per year coupons are paid:

$$D = (1/R) + \tau - \frac{(1+R/m)+(CR-R)N/m}{CR(1+R/m)^N - (CR-R)}. \qquad (5.3)$$

For the bond analyzed here, $R = 0.12$; $CR = 0.10$; $\tau = 0.5$; $N = 10$; and $m = 2$. Thus, from equation (5.3),

$$D = (1/0.12) + 0.5 - \frac{(1.06)+(0.10-0.12)5}{0.10(1.06)^{10} - (0.10-0.12)}$$

$= 4.01$ years (or 8.02 semiannual periods).

Since the five-year, 10 percent coupon bond yielding 12 percent we have been discussing has a duration of 4.01 years, its risk characteristics will closely mimic those of a 12 percent yield four-year maturity discount bond. In particular, they would have nearly identical percentage price changes for a given change in yield.

For example, suppose that immediately after purchase, the yields on both the five-year, 10 percent coupon bond and a four-year discount bond each rose by 0.5 percent. The price of the coupon bond would fall by \$16.82 to \$909.08: a 1.870 percent fall in value. In response to the same 12 percent to 12.5 percent yield rise, the price of the discount bond would fall 1.867 percent from \$627.41 to \$615.70.

The price elasticity application of duration also can be illustrated from this example. The five-year, 10 percent coupon bond initially had a duration of 4.01 years. Since a bond's duration equals its price elasticity with respect to a small change in the discount factor, a one percent rise (fall) in the discount factor $(1+R)$ will lead to a D percent fall (rise) in the value of the bond:

$$\Delta P/P = -D\Delta R/(1+R). \qquad (5.4)$$

The rise in the yield from 1.12 to 1.125 $(0.005/1.12 = 0.45\%)$ is predicted to bring about a 1.79 percent fall in the bond's value (0.45 percent multiplied by 4.01). This prediction matches up well with the actual percentage price change of 1.87 percent. A small prediction error will occur, however, since the duration is the true elasticity only for infinitesimal discount factor changes. (For greater than "infinitesimal" discount factor movements, the true elasticity does not remain constant.)

Viewed from an alternative perspective, the fact that the five-year bond currently has a 4.01-year duration means that its 12 percent yield to maturity is "guaranteed" over a four-year horizon. Consider a once and for all shift in the yield structure such as the 12 percent to 12.5 percent rise discussed above. While the bond's market value initially drops, reinvestment income on the coupons received throughout the bond's life will be higher than initially expected. If the bond is held to maturity, the accumulated value as of the end of the five-year holding period consists of the \$1,000 redemption value, the \$500 in coupons, and the \$116.83 income from reinvesting the coupons at 12.5 percent. This will exceed the total return at 12 percent of \$1,609.04. The bond's actual yield to maturity will exceed its initial yield to maturity. Conversely, if yields had fallen such that reinvestment income was lower than had been anticipated, the bond's actual yield to maturity would have been lower than initially expected.

Whether the initial yield is actually received over a given holding period depends on which of the two opposing factors dominates: the effect on market value or the effect on reinvestment income. A rise in yields will lead to a fall in the market value of a bond; however, a rise in yields will also lead to higher than anticipated reinvestment income. For short holding periods, market risk outweighs reinvestment risk; for long holding periods, reinvestment risk outweighs market risk. In this context, a bond's duration is the holding period for which the bond's market risk is just offset by its reinvestment risk. For a holding period ending beyond the bond's duration point, reinvestment risk outweighs market risk: An increase in yield raises reinvestment proceeds by more than enough to make up for the market value decline. Conversely, for a holding period ending prior to the bond's duration point, market risk outweighs reinvestment risk: An increase in yield lowers market value by more than the induced increase in the coupon reinvestment income. For a holding period just *equal* to the bond's initial duration, the initial yield to maturity is received regardless of whether an increase or decrease in yields occurs. This property plays an important role in the immunization strategies to be discussed below. It also again makes the correspondence between a coupon bond and a discount bond with a maturity equal to the coupon bond's duration meaningful: Both have zero return risk over a holding period equal to the coupon bond's duration.

Table 5–2 presents a sample of alternative maturity, coupon and yield combinations, and the durations of the associated bonds. Note

Table 5–2.   Alternative Bonds and Their Durations.

Term to maturity (years)	Coupon rate	Yield to maturity	Duration
5	0	12.00	5.00
5	10	8.00	4.09
5	10	12.00	4.01
10	8	8.00	7.07
10	8	12.00	6.61
10	12	12.00	6.08
20	8	8.00	10.29
20	8	12.00	8.53
20	12	12.00	7.98

especially the fact that the only bond for which duration corresponds to term to maturity is the zero coupon (i.e., "pure discount") bond.

USE OF DURATION IN IMMUNIZATION STRATEGIES

Duration is currently used by investment officers as a guide in managing the risk in fixed-income portfolios. By altering the duration of assets and liabilities, the firm's net yield sensitivity can be increased or decreased in a manner consistent with interest rate expectations. In particular, for the firm desiring only to minimize risk exposure, *immunization* strategies designed to create equal and offsetting interest rate sensitivities for assets and liabilities are appropriate. It is of interest to note that cash market immunization strategies were first proposed in the early 1950s by a British actuary, F. M. Redington, who was concerned with life insurance company investment risk management.

Whether the firm wishes to maintain some exposure to interest risk or complete immunization is desired, dynamic portfolio management strategies incorporating the duration concept are very useful for optimal results. The use of futures contracts can provide the investment officer important flexibility in implementing such strategies. As a prelude to discussing how futures can be integrated into immunization strategies, we first present a brief review of the elements of a simple cash market strategy for comparative purposes.

Suppose that the firm is considering a deal in which it will invest $10 million in a ten-year, 11 percent coupon bond and fund it with a five-year, $10 million face value liability contract at 9 percent. Assume that both securities are currently priced at par: The investment is fully funded. The manager wishes to measure the net interest rate risk to the firm resulting from the "unmatched" asset/liability structure of this proposed deal. The net risk from small movements in interest rates of both the bond asset (V_B) and the liability (V_L) can be evaluated through the duration-based elasticity expression (5.4). Their dollar changes in response to changes in their respective yields are given by equations (5.5) and (5.6):

$$\Delta V_B = -D_B V_B \Delta R_B / (1 + R_B); \tag{5.5}$$

$$\Delta V_L = -D_L V_L \Delta R_L / (1 + R_L). \tag{5.6}$$

For the position to be immunized, its net market value must not be changed by a shift in yields, which implies that $\Delta V_B = \Delta V_L$, or

$$D_B V_B \Delta R_B/(1+R_B) = D_L V_L \Delta R_L/(1+R_L), \qquad (5.7)$$

Since the asset and liability have equal value, this immunization condition simplifies to

$$D_B \Delta R_B/(1+R_B) = D_L \Delta R_L/(1+R_L). \qquad (5.8)$$

Equation (5.8) makes clear the general principle that the proper immunizing strategy depends on the way in which yields of assets and liabilities are assumed to change in relation to each other. If an interest rate change results in an equal *percentage* change in discount factors — that is,

$$\Delta R_B/(1+R_B) = \Delta R_L/(1+R_L),$$

then the proper immunizing strategy will be to simply match durations of the asset and liability sides $(D_B = D_L)$.

With this yield shift, the actual net dollar risk of the deal depends on the degree to which the durations are mismatched. As currently structured, the deal has a net interest rate risk equivalent to that of a long position in a 2.17-year pure discount bond since, at their current yields, the duration of the ten-year, 11 percent coupon bond asset is 6.30 years, while the duration of five-year, 10 percent coupon liability is 4.13 years, for a difference in the net duration overall of $6.30 - 4.13 = 2.17$. Thus, the value of this deal to the firm will rise (fall) if interest rates fall (rise), by the same percent as a 2.17-year pure discount bond.

The interest rate risk of the bond/liability package may or may not be acceptable to the firm's investment officer in light of the yield spread obtained. He might wish to restructure the deal to reduce, or even eliminate, the existing interest rate risk. This could be done by shortening the duration of the asset side and/or lengthening the duration of the liability side. The immunizing strategy here would be to match the durations of assets and liabilities. This could be accomplished either through a new combination of cash market securities or, as will be developed below, through positions in financial future contracts.

One direct immunization strategy is to change the asset mix of the deal. This could be done by placing a fraction of the funds into, for example, one-year zero coupon bonds or Treasury bills so as to match the dollar value interest rate sensitivities of the deal's asset and liability components. Consistent with the flat yield curve assumption, assume that these one-year bonds are currently priced at $898 per $1,000 face to yield 11 percent. Since these one-year bonds are zero coupon securities, their duration equals their one-year term to maturity. In order to match the value sensitivity of the liability contract, \$4.094 million (40.94 percent) of assets should be shifted from the ten-year bonds to the one-year bonds. The duration of the asset portfolio would then be

$$D_{\text{assets}} = [V_{10}/(V_{10} + V_1)]D_{10} + [V_1/(V_{10} + V_1)]D_1;$$

$$= (0.5906)(6.3) + (0.4094)(1)$$

$$= 4.13 \text{ years}, \tag{5.9}$$

where V_{10} and V_1 are the amounts invested in the ten-year and one-year securities, and D_{10} and D_1 are their respective durations.

This matches the duration of the liability side. Under the assumption that relative yield shifts are proportional, the sensitivity of the asset side to interest rate changes now exactly offsets that of the liability side. Thus, an immunized deal would consist of \$5.906 million in the ten-year bonds, \$4.094 million in the one-year bonds (i.e., face value of \$4.544 million) and \$10 million of the five-year liability contract funding. Such a strategy, if appropriately rebalanced over time, would be expected to lock in the original 1 percent yield spread over a 4.13-year holding period.

Some qualifications to this simple immunization example are in order. First, the strategy employed actually only provides protection over the next instant of time. Both as time passes and as yields ultimately do change, the durations of the assets and liabilities will become mismatched. To keep the portfolio immunized it should be monitored continually and rebalanced whenever necessary to reflect the changing price sensitivities of the component securities. Otherwise, the anticipated asset/liability yield spread will be exposed to risk from market yield fluctuations.

Second, the example constructed above assumed a flat yield curve. The assumption that a single per period discount factor is appropriate for valuation is at odds with the observed shape of the term structure of zero coupon yields. Since a coupon bond can be viewed as a portfolio of discount bonds, the yield to maturity on a coupon bond is a complex average of these zero coupon yields. A more sophisticated analysis in the face of ascending, descending, or hump-shaped yield curves would utilize the exact set of per period discount factors to compute durations, as in equation (5.1).

Third, a most crucial factor for determining the proper immunizing strategy in the example examined above was the assumption that the asset and liability yield shifts were exactly proportional to each other.

Duration matching will not accomplish immunization if the yield shifts are not really proportional.[1] For example, if the asset/liability yield shift pattern was more accurately described as equal changes in basis points ($\Delta R_B = \Delta R_L$, instead of $\Delta R_B/1 + R_B = \Delta R_L/1 + R_L$), the immunization condition would be

$$D_B/1 + R_B = D_L/1 + R_L, \qquad (5.10)$$

a matching of weighted or "modified" Macauley durations.

Finally, regardless of the form of the best average relationship between asset and liability yield shifts (and, therefore, the specific form of the immunizing condition), the fact that yields are not perfectly correlated implies that even continuously rebalanced immunization strategies will leave some degree of risk. Neither cash-based nor futures-based (see below) immunization strategies will be perfectly "immune" to interest rate risk.

A FUTURES-BASED IMMUNIZATION STRATEGY

In the last example, an immunization strategy using financial futures instead of shifting assets from long- to short-term bonds could have been employed to eliminate the initial 2.17-year duration gap in the original deal. In general, long or short futures positions can be added to any portfolio to attain a desired interest rate risk exposure. For example, in order to offset the duration gap present in the original asset/liability contract package, the investment officer could short thirty-one six-month to delivery Treasury bond futures contracts currently priced at 74.19.

The first step in deriving the appropriate Treasury bond futures position for this immunizing hedge involves computing the futures contract's duration. The duration of a futures contract differs slightly from that for cash securities. It is calculated as the duration of the underlying cheapest deliverable security using (1) the current futures

---

1. For a discussion of immunization strategies in the presence of more sophisticated yield comovement patterns see the collection of papers in George Kaufman, Gerald Bierwag, and Alden Toevs, eds., *Innovations in Bond Portfolio Management* (Greenwich, Conn.: JAI Press, 1983). A more accessible source for a first pass at some of these issues is Stephen Schaefer, "Immunization and Duration: A Review of Theory, Performance, and Applications," *Midland Corporate Finance Journal* (Fall 1984).

price, (2) the conversion factor for that security, and (3) the contract's delivery date as the relevant date from which to date the deliverable security's remaining cash flows and to derive the implied futures yield to maturity. First, one calculates the adjusted futures price (the futures settlement price multiplied by the deliverable bond's conversion factor). Next, one computes an implied yield to maturity for the cash bond using this adjusted futures price and the bond's cash flow *as viewed from the expected delivery date* of the futures contract. Finally, the bond's duration as of the expected delivery date is calculated using this adjusted yield. Except for these differences, the mechanics of the calculation are identical to those for cash security duration computations based on equation (5.3). In principle, we are merely taking the duration of the futures contract to be the duration of the deliverable bond as of the expected delivery date at that bond's current forward price.[2]

For example, in the problem above, suppose that the actual cheapest-to-deliver issue was a 7 percent coupon, twenty-five-year to maturity issue that was priced at 66.137 to yield 11 percent. For delivery against a six-month to maturity futures contract, this bond would have a conversion factor of 0.8933 (based on a 24.5-year maturity). The futures price is assumed to be 74.191; the adjusted futures price is 66.275 (= 0.8933 × 74.191). The adjusted yield to maturity based upon the adjusted futures price and the cash flows of the 24.5-year bond is 11 percent. (This is a flat yield curve example, and the futures quote used has its "correct" no-arbitrage value.) Finally, through equation (5.3), the duration of the futures contract is 9.52 years.

The immunizing futures position is obtained by dividing the original portfolio's dollar-weighted duration gap by the dollar-weighted duration of one ($100,000 face) futures contract. This solution assumes proportional yield changes for all three components: the bond, the liability contract, and, implicitly, the cheapest-to-deliver bond underlying the futures. In order to reduce the duration and the interest rate risk of the original portfolio a *short* futures position that fills the dollar-weighted duration gap must be taken so that

---

2. One technical, but probably not too important, qualification to the method outlined above for calculating the duration of the futures contract should be mentioned. Use of the adjusted futures price (as computed using the current market futures quote) in place of the true forward price of the cheapest deliverable bond is not strictly exact. The converted futures price in practice typically understates the true forward bond price because of the value of delivery options that the Treasury bond futures contract grants holders of short positions.

$$D_F(N_F V_F) + D_B V_B - D_L V_L = 0,$$

where V_F represents the value of a futures contract. This gives

$$N_F = -[D_B V_B - D_L V_L]/D_F V_F$$

$$= -[(6.30)(\$10 \text{ million}) - (4.13)(\$10 \text{ million})]/(9.52)(\$74{,}191)$$

$$= -30.72 \sim 31 \text{ contracts short.} \tag{5.11}$$

DURATION-BASED HEDGING OF THE FOUR BOND TREASURY PORTFOLIO

To give a more concrete illustration of the duration-based technique for futures hedge construction, the four-bond portfolio of Treasuries analyzed in Chapter 4 will be reexamined. Suppose the goal of the hedge program is to choose a futures position that completely eliminates the interest rate risk of the Treasury bond portfolio in the immediate future. The hedge should be structured such that the dollar-weighted yield sensitivity of the total hedged position equals zero. As before, we assume a flat yield curve and equal proportional yield shifts for all four bonds and the underlying cheapest deliverable issue. In this problem, there are no interest sensitive liabilities explicitly considered, but the asset position to be hedged consists of *four* bonds. The futures position formula introduced above should be altered by dropping the liability component and adding three additional bond components. Thus, the proper number of futures contracts to short to hedge this position will be the sum of the contract positions necessary to hedge each of the four individual bond positions in the portfolio:

$$N_F = [\Sigma - D_{B_i}(V_{B_i})]/D_F V_F. \tag{5.12}$$

To calculate the hedge position that would immunize the portfolio, it is necessary to compute the durations of each of the four bonds and of the relevant March 1984 futures contract as of the 30 December 1983 inception of the hedge. (We again follow the rule of only hedging with the near, non-delivery month contract.) These durations, along with the relevant value data, are presented in Table 5-3. The 8.88-year duration of the futures contract was calculated using the following inputs for equation (5.3): $R = 0.1157$; $\tau = 0.378$; $CR = 0.07625$; $N = 46$; and $m = 2$. These inputs reflect the characteristics of the 7⅝s of February 2007, which we have assumed to be the cheapest

Table 5-3. Hedging the Four-Bond Treasury Portfolio:
Duration Computations, Dollar Weightings, and Solution.

Bond	Duration	Price	Accrued interest	Value	Duration × value
13.75 MAY 1992	5.43	109.594	1.624	111.218	603.91
10.375 MAY 1995	6.56	91.281	1.296	92.577	607.31
11.75 FEB 2001	8.31	98.594	4.363	102.957	855.57
14 NOV 2011	7.36	116.812	1.749	118.561	872.61
Futures	8.88	70.0312			

$$N_F = (\Sigma - D_i V_i)/D_F V_F$$
$$= (-2{,}939.4 \times 50{,}000)/(8.88 \times 70.0312 \times 1{,}000)$$
$$= -236.33 \sim 236 \text{ contracts short.}$$

deliverable issue for the March 1984 bond contract as of December 1983. The conversion factor for this issue was 0.9646. Using the adjusted futures price of 67.552 (= 0.9646 × 70.0312) implies a yield for this issue equal to 0.1157 as of the assumed 30 March 1984 delivery date. A size factor of 50,000/1,000 = 50 is employed since that is the ratio of face value to contract size for each cash bond in the portfolio relative to the future.

The analysis reveals that the (current) immunizing futures position for this Treasury bond portfolio is one that is short 236 contracts. Notice that the hedge constructed here is identical to the solution given in Chapter 4 for this same four-bond portfolio problem. The correspondence should be clear in view of the price/yield elasticity concept upon which duration is based. Of course, this 236 contract short hedge has to be rebalanced both as yields change and time passes in order to keep its (expected) zero interest rate risk structure. Also notice that, since the "horizon" of this hedge is really only the next instant (day) of time, no "tail" is needed.

Immunizing a Treasury Portfolio Funded by a Guaranteed Interest Contract

As we discussed in the previous chapter, guaranteed interest contracts (GICs), which offer the purchaser (often a pension fund) a guaranteed return over a specific investment horizon (typically, five years), have become important products for the insurance industry. In contrast to the "liability contract" analyzed earlier, most GIC transactions also include an offering or commitment period prior to the actual transfer of funds from the purchaser, during which the issuing insurance company is at risk since investment yields could fall and substantially reduce profit margins. Further, because GICs are priced very competitively, issuing insurance companies usually choose to invest the acquired funds in bonds with longer maturities and/or lower quality rating in order to attain an adequate yield spread. Thus, the GIC issuer typically is subject to three types of risk: (1) initial offering period investment yield risk; (2) reinvestment risk on the coupons received from the ultimate bond asset position; and (3) holding-period price risk on the bond position due to its usually "unmatched" maturity and/or credit quality characteristics.[3] The duration-based immunization strategy is one approach to managing the risks posed by a GIC-funded investment portfolio. This strategy would involve financial futures positions during the GIC offering period and combined futures/cash positions throughout the remainder of the GIC's life. As before, the exact positions would be chosen in both pre- and post-funding periods to match the dollar-weighted durations of the asset and liability sides of the portfolio.

For example, suppose on 30 December 1983 an insurer and its pension fund client commit to a five-year, zero coupon, $35 million face value GIC to be closed in three months at $21.49 million (an implied yield of 10 percent). The insurer plans to invest the deferred $21.49 million of funds in the four-bond Treasury portfolio considered above. Take-down of the GIC commitment and purchase of the asset portfolio will occur on 30 March 1984. The insurer desires to immunize the net interest rate risk of the deal. As usual, the "simple" flat term structure and equal proportional yield shift risk structure will be assumed. The immunizing strategy is to set the dollar-weighted net duration of the portfolio equal to zero. However, it is convenient to view the problem as trying to use futures contracts to make the duration of the assets plus futures equal to that of the GIC "target."

As of the beginning of the commitment period, the insurer is holding a GIC to be sold in three months and has a planned purchase of the Treasury bond portfolio at that time. Thus, the insurer's initial

---

3. A fourth type is the "take-down" risk inherent in the commitment if the purchaser of the GIC contract is not legally obligated to complete the transaction.

portfolio is best described as a long forward position in the GIC (to be offset through its sale in three months) and a short forward position in the Treasury bonds (to be similarly offset in three months by the cash market bond investment). Thus, the futures hedges will be "anticipatory" in nature. The duration-based hedge ratios have to be adjusted to account for the deferred settlement of the securities involved. Because both the GIC and Treasury bond positions are deferred delivery or "forward" positions, their durations should be calculated as of their three-month-ahead acquisition date. Similar to the adjustment explained earlier to calculate the duration of a futures contract, the values of the bonds and the GIC are adjusted to equal their implied *forward values*. Under a flat yield curve environment, their forward values would be those at which, in three month's time, the securities would earn their initial yield. Thus, the forward values of the four Treasury bonds under the flat yield curve assumption can be calculated as 114.48, 13.75 May 1992; 95.25, 10.375 May 1995; 100.10, 11.75 Feb 2001; and 122.03, 14 Nov 2011. In a more general yield curve environment, the appropriate implied forward yield for investment in three months' time should be used to determine the bond's current forward value.

Through the methods previously outlined, and with these additional adjustments, the current durations of the forward GIC (five years) and forward Treasury bond portfolio can be calculated (13.75 May 1992, $D = 5.04$; 10.375 May 1995, $D = 6.38$; 11.75 Feb 2001, $D = 7.54$; 14 Nov 2011, $D = 8.06$). It is convenient to compute the duration of the total forward Treasury bond portfolio position. To calculate the forward portfolio's duration, weight each of the individual durations by the percent of total forward value each bond position contributes. Specifically,

$$D = (0.265)(5.04) + (0.221)(6.38) + (0.232)(7.54) + (0.283)(8.06)$$

$$= 6.77 \text{ years.}$$

Thus, as the duration of the short forward bond position is 1.77 years greater than that of the long forward GIC position, the dollar-weighted negative duration gap of the deal must be closed with a *long* futures contract position in order to achieve immunization. As before, the duration of the March 1984 futures contract is 8.88. The number of futures contracts to be traded to fill the duration gap is

$$N_F = (6.77 - 5)\$21.49 \text{ million}/(8.88)(\$70,031.2)$$

$$= 61.17 \sim 61 \text{ contracts long.}$$

This position must be "tailed," as the futures contracts will realize cash flows over the three-month commitment period, while the forwards will not. The interest sensitivities implicitly have been equalized as of the closing date. The tail is determined by the expected interest rate over the horizon of the three-month hedge. If the expected interest rate for the three-month commitment period also is 11 percent semiannual, the tailed position would be

$$N_F = (1/1.055)^{0.50}(61.17)$$
$$= 59.55 \sim 60 \text{ contracts long.}$$

This procedure for setting up an anticipatory hedge of the GIC commitment differs from what was suggested in the last chapter in that we are now taking explicit account of the risk characteristics of the GIC liability in addition to the bonds that are to be purchased. The reason for this difference is that, in the current context, this hedge is part of an immunizing strategy. The objective of the previous hedge was to fix a yield on the long-term bonds, while here it is to fix the yield *differential* between the bonds and the GIC liability.

Throughout the offering period, the long futures position remains the only component of the portfolio actually transacted. However, it should be updated if yields change sufficiently to alter the relative dollar sensitivities of the hedge components. Regardless, at the closing of the cash market transactions at the end of the three-month offering period, the futures component of the portfolio must undergo a dramatic reversal in order to maintain immunization. It is not enough merely to close out the long futures position; a new net short contract position must be initiated in order to immunize the risk inherent during the remaining five-year life of the four Treasury bond/GIC portfolio. The offering period hedge was not the only important risk imposed by this "unmatched" deal. The new appropriate futures position would be calculated in the same manner as the immunizing example of the previous section. Also, the proper futures position would have to be periodically reevaluated in light of duration drift, and the futures contracts would have to be "rolled-over" in order to keep the immunizing properties of the hedge intact. In particular, the proper immunizing futures position would change throughout the period because of the different aging characteristics of the long-term versus shorter term securities (the Treasury bonds versus the GIC).

6 HEDGING EQUITY POSITIONS WITH STOCK INDEX FUTURES

Many life insurance companies hold sizable positions in stock, often in separate accounts which allow greater flexibility. The stock index futures markets offer a number of attractive possibilities for improving risk management and for enhancing returns in equity investments. Hedging with index futures also involves features unique to the stock market. In this chapter we will describe the stock index contracts and a number of the most important uses of this versatile instrument.

MARKET AND NONMARKET RISK

Modern portfolio theory, as it has been developed over the last twenty years, emphasizes that the effective risk on a stock depends on what other stocks are held. As different stocks are combined in investment portfolios, some risk—that associated with events specific to a single firm or industry—tends to be diversified away. For example, if in one year General Motors loses market share to Ford, GM stock may do relatively poorly while Ford stock will perform better than expected. This possibility contributes to variability of returns for each company's shares. But an investor who held a portfolio containing both Ford and GM would not experience this profit variability for the two firms as risk. Because the losses on his GM would be offset by the extra gains on Ford, the effect of this firm specific risk is diversified away in his overall portfolio.

Similarly, holding a broad spectrum of stocks will tend to eliminate the impact of risks associated with individual industries. In general, some industries will perform worse than expected and others will perform better, with the differences relative to the overall market tending to smooth themselves out within a balanced portfolio.

However, all stocks are exposed to the effects of broad market forces like war and peace, changes in interest rates and in the general level of economic activity, changes in tax laws, and so on. While some stocks are more influenced by such phenomena than others, all will be affected to some degree. This type of risk can not be diversified away by holding stocks in portfolios, because nearly every stock tends to move along with the market, at least to some extent.

Modern portfolio theory in the form of the capital asset pricing model (CAPM) divides the total risk on an individual stock into a "firm specific" or "unsystematic" component, which can be eliminated through diversification, and a "market" or "systematic" component, which cannot. Only the market risk component is considered relevant in determining how investors will price stocks in the market because they diversify away the firm specific risk.

The measure of market risk is a stock's "beta." Beta (β) is defined as the covariance between a stock's return and the return on the overall market, divided by the variance of return on the market. For some stock i, this can be written

$$\beta_i = \text{cov}[R_i, R_m]/\text{var}[R_m], \qquad (6.1)$$

where R_m refers to the return on the "market" portfolio (i.e., a portfolio consisting of all stocks held together).

Notice the similarity between this expression for beta and the definition given above in equation (2.5) for the risk-minimizing hedge ratio for a futures hedge. The only difference is that here the return on the futures contract is replaced by the return on the market portfolio. We will come back to this point below when we discuss hedge ratios for index futures hedges.

Like the risk-minimizing hedge ratio, beta can be estimated by regression on past data. Given a series of observed returns over time for stock i (R_{it}) and for the market (R_{mt}) (inclusive of dividends), running the following linear regression

$$R_{it} = a + bR_{mt} + \epsilon_{it} \tag{6.2}$$

yields the coefficient b as the estimate of stock i's beta. (The term ϵ_{it}, of course, refers to the regression residual.)

The CAPM relates the rate of return that can be expected on stock i to its exposure to market risk, as measured by its beta. In equilibrium every stock, or portfolio of stocks, should be priced in the market so that

$$\bar{R}_i = r + \beta_i(\bar{R}_m - r), \tag{6.3}$$

where $\bar{R}_i$ is the expected return on stock i, r is the return on a riskless investment such as a Treasury bill, and $\bar{R}_m$ is the expected return on the market portfolio.

This familiar equation has become widely accepted as the premier model of market equilibrium in the securities markets. Performance of portfolio managers is routinely measured relative to the betas of their portfolios, and much research effort is devoted to procedures for estimating betas more accurately than by the simple regression shown in equation (6.2).

Clearly, the beta of the market portfolio itself must be 1.0. Imagine the result in equation (6.2) of regressing the returns of the market on itself. Or it can also be seen directly in equation (6.1), since $\text{cov}[R_m, R_m] = \text{var}[R_m]$. The beta of a riskless security is zero. Lastly, the beta of a portfolio is equal to the weighted average of the betas of the individual stocks in the portfolio, where the weight on stock i's beta is proportional to the dollar amount invested in stock i.

$$\beta_p = \sum_{i=1}^{N} w_i \beta_i. \tag{6.4}$$

Example: Assume the following data for IBM and ATT:

	IBM	ATT
Price	110	16
Beta	1.05	0.80

The portfolio consisting of 1,000 shares of IBM and 5,000 shares of ATT has a value of $(1,000)(110) + (5,000)(16) = 110,000 + 80,000 = \$190,000$. Its beta is

$$\frac{110,000}{190,000}(1.05) + \frac{80,000}{190,000}(0.80) = 0.945.$$

As a special case of this result, consider portfolios made up only of investments in the market portfolio and the risk free asset. If the fraction of the funds invested in the market portfolio is X and the remainder, $(1-X)$ is invested in the risk free securities, the portfolio's beta will be $(X)(1.0)+(1-X)(0)=X$ — that is, the beta is just equal to the fraction invested in the market.

Now consider the expected return on this portfolio, which will be the weighted average of the relevant returns, $\bar{R}_p=(X)\bar{R}_m+(1-X)r$. But this can be written as the return on the riskless asset plus X times the risk premium on the market.

$$\bar{R}_p=r+X(\bar{R}_m-r),$$

and since the beta of this portfolio is equal to X, we have

$$\bar{R}_p=r+\beta_p(\bar{R}_m-r). \tag{6.5}$$

The expected return on this portfolio made up of investments in the market portfolio and the risk free asset is equal to the risk free interest rate plus the portfolio's beta times the premium by which the return on the stock market is expected to exceed the risk free rate.

This is just equation (6.3) again. But its significance is that we have just shown how any investor can create a portfolio with whatever beta he likes from just investments in the market portfolio and risk free securities, and this portfolio must yield the rate of return implied by the CAPM. In considering any other stocks or portfolios of stocks, one should bear in mind that if they do not earn at least the return specified by equation (6.3) one can expect to do better for the same level of market risk by holding the market portfolio and riskless securities.

Because market risk cannot be eliminated by diversification, possibilities for risk management in stock portfolios in the past were fairly limited. To reduce a portfolio's beta, there were really only two choices. First, one could invest only in stocks that had low betas. This naturally led to a portfolio whose weighted average beta was also low. But there is a limit to the amount of risk reduction that can be achieved in this way, since there are almost no stocks whose betas are negative and, in fact, very few below about 0.6. Further, as the number of different stocks held is reduced so as to include only those with the lowest betas, the effect of diversification tends to diminish and firm specific risk reappears as a problem for the portfolio.

The second way to reduce market risk traditionally was by selling stocks entirely and investing in fixed-income securities. If stocks were replaced by long-term bonds in the portfolio, this had the effect of reducing beta at the cost of increasing exposure to interest rate risk. To avoid this problem, money market instruments had to be purchased in place of stocks.

The advent of stock index futures greatly expanded and simplified the possibilities for managing market risk in stock portfolios. The idea of an index futures contract is to provide a mechanism for fixing a return on the market portfolio. This allows a portfolio manager to alter the market risk on his portfolio without changing its composition. It can be done simply, directly, and with very low transactions costs relative to the alternative strategies.

Why does a portfolio manager alter the market exposure of his investments? There are several general reasons. One is simply to reduce the overall risk level. A conservative investment philosophy might entail setting a target risk level comparable to that on a portfolio that was half-invested in stocks and half in bonds. With index futures available, any stock portfolio can be hedged so as to yield the desired beta, regardless of the betas of the individual stocks.

A second reason to alter a portfolio's beta is to engage in "market timing"—in other words, to reduce its exposure to market risk when the stock market is expected to go down and to increase it when the market is expected to rise. If successful, this strategy can increase overall returns considerably. Market timing is greatly facilitated by stock index futures, since the beta can be adjusted directly without the need to buy or sell individual stocks. That may be difficult to do quickly or at reasonable prices in the case of less liquid issues.

Finally, a portfolio manager who feels that certain stocks are underpriced relative to the market might wish to concentrate his purchases on them and reduce the beta of the resulting portfolio by selling stock index futures. This has the effect of increasing the impact of relative performance on the overall return on the portfolio.

These are a few of the most important strategies involving stock index futures. Another is buying or selling index futures in advance of the purchase or sale of actual stocks in order to take advantage of a currently attractive level of the market. The manager then gains time to make more careful transactions in the markets for the individual shares. Index futures may also be used to hedge the impact of market fluctuations on company's future issuance of its own equity. Examples of these uses will be presented and discussed below.

THE MARKET INDEXES

There are currently futures contracts trading on three broad market indexes: the Standard and Poor's 500 (S&P), the New York Stock Exchange Composite (NYSE), and the Value Line Average (VLA). Two other contracts based on narrower indexes are also being traded: the Standard and Poor's 100 and the Major Market Index (MMI). Other stock index contracts have been proposed already and may be traded in the future.

In addition to differences between stock indexes due to coverage of different stocks, there are several different ways to construct an index that are currently in use. Naturally the way an index is calculated affects the pricing and risk characteristics of a futures contract based on that index.

All indexes share certain features in common. Each specifies a set of securities to be covered, although periodically changes may need to be made, because of new listings, mergers and bankruptcies, and similar events. Technical adjustments are generally needed when the group of stocks included in the index is altered or when there is a capitalization change such as a stock split. Every index begins with a base period, for which the index is defined to be equal to some given value, such as 100.00. And every index involves a rule for combining the returns or prices of the stocks it contains to determine the value of the index subsequent to the base period.

Table 6–1 illustrates four different types of index. We use just two stocks: ABC, with 1,000 shares outstanding and priced at 80 on 2 January, the chosen base period, and XYZ, with 400 shares, initially priced at 50.

One of the simplest kinds of index is an equally weighted index of returns. It is computed by taking the total return since the base period on each stock, averaging them, and applying the result to the base value. That is,

$$I_t = \frac{\sum_{i=1}^{N} (P_{it}/P_{i0})}{N} \times I_0 \tag{6.6}$$

where I_t is the index for date t,
             I_0 is the base value of the index,

Table 6-1. Alternative Types of Stock Index.

Number of shares outstanding: ABC/1,000; XYZ/400

	2 Jan.	3 Jan.	4 Jan.
ABC Price	80	82	81
XYZ Price	50	54	49
Indexes			
Equally weighted returns index	100	105.25	99.63
Equally weighted price index	100	104.62	100.00
Market value weighted index	100	103.60	100.60
Equally weighted geometric average index	100	105.21	99.61

P_{it}, P_{i0} are the date t and initial date prices for stock i, and N is the total number of stocks in the index.

Example: The 3 January, equally weighted returns index is calculated as follows:

$$I_{\text{Jan. 3}} = \frac{(82/80) + (54/50)}{2} \times 100.00 = 105.25.$$

Although this kind of index has the reasonable property that each stock's return is weighted equally, so far there is no stock index futures contract based on an equally weighted returns index.

A variant of this method that has an historical precedent is the equally weighted price index. This index is simply the average of the *prices* for all included stocks divided by the average price in the base period and multiplied by the base index value.

$$I_t = \frac{\sum_{i=1}^{N} P_{it}}{\sum_{i=1}^{N} P_{0t}} \times I_0, \tag{6.7}$$

where the definitions are as before.

Example: The 3 January equally weighted price index is calculated as follows:

$$I_{\text{Jan. 3}} = \frac{82 + 54}{80 + 50} = 104.62.$$

The Dow Jones Index is an example of an equally weighted price index. While there is no futures contract on the Dow, the Major Market Index, devised by the American Stock Exchange as the underlying index for one of its index options contracts, is computed in this way in order to give it a similar character to the Dow Jones Index. A futures contract based on the MMI has recently been introduced at the Chicago Board of Trade.

Large capitalization firms like IBM have a much greater impact on the performance of the average investor's portfolio than do small firms, but the first two indexes weighted each stock equally. Many indexes take differences in firm size into account by weighting the returns on individual stocks by their total market value. This gives IBM relatively more weight than smaller companies. A market value weighted index is computed as follows:

$$I_t = \frac{\sum_{i=1}^{N} S_i P_{it}}{\sum_{i=1}^{N} S_i P_{i0}} \times I_0,$$
(6.8)

where S_i is the number of outstanding shares for stock i.

Example: The 3 January market value weighted index is calculated as follows:

$$I_{\text{Jan. }3} = \frac{(1,000)(82) + (400)(54)}{(1,000)(80) + (400)(50)} \times 100.00 = 103.60.$$

The majority of stock indexes are market value weighted indexes, including both the Standard and Poor's 500 and the New York Stock Exchange Composite.

One final type of index is an equally weighted geometric average. Here each stock's return from the previous day is computed, these are combined by geometric averaging, and the resulting return is applied to yesterday's index to get today's. That is,

$$I_t = \sqrt[N]{(P_{1t}/P_{1t-1}) \times (P_{2t}/P_{2t-1}) \times \cdots \times (P_{Nt}/P_{Nt-1})} \times I_{t-1},$$
(6.9)

where $\sqrt[N]{\bullet}$ denotes the operation of taking the Nth root.

Example: The 3 January and 4 January index values of this type are calculated as follows:

$$I_{\text{Jan. }3} = \sqrt{(82/80) \times (54/50)} \times 100.00 = 105.21.$$

$$I_{\text{Jan. }4} = \sqrt{(81/82) \times (49/54)} \times 105.21 = 99.61.$$

The major index of this sort is the Value Line Index. The Kansas City Board of Trade trades a futures contract on this index. It was, in fact, the first stock index futures contract to be introduced, starting in February 1982. One peculiar feature of this kind of index is that while individual stock returns are weighted equally as in the first index discussed, because of a mathematical property of geometric averaging, this index will always be lower than or at most equal to one based on an equally weighted simple average of returns if they have the same base value.

The "market portfolio" as it is customarily used in portfolio theory inherently refers to a portfolio that has the same portfolio proportions as the total supply of all shares issued by all firms. One might think of it as having the same composition as a huge mutual fund that owned every individual share of stock in existence. In this portfolio, each firm's weight would be equal to its total market value divided by the total market value of all firms together. That is, the market portfolio is best represented by a value weighted index.

Both the Standard and Poor's 500 index and the New York Stock Exchange Composite are broad, value weighted indexes. The S&P contains 500 of the largest and best known companies, nearly all of which are traded on the New York Stock Exchange and are therefore included in the NYSE index as well. Because of market value weighting, IBM, the largest capitalization stock, has a weight in the index of about 6 percent, while the number 500 firm receives less than 0.005 percent. The base period for the S&P index is the average of stock prices during the years 1941–43, and the level of the index for that period is defined to be 10.0. As membership in the index changes due to mergers, bankruptcies, the AT&T breakup, and so on, the base value is adjusted in such a way that the return on the index for the date that the composition of the index changes reflects the change in value of the new index portfolio. Thus, continuity is retained.

The NYSE index is a broader index, containing all U.S. stocks traded on the exchange — over 1,500 at present. Because of value weighting again, the stocks contained in the S&P index receive over 75 percent of the weight in the NYSE. Not surprisingly, the two indexes are highly correlated with one another.

Both the S&P and NYSE indexes are good proxies for the market portfolio of theory. Although there are many more stocks in existence than the ones included in these indexes, they do contain the largest capitalization companies. The NYSE stocks would comprise more than 85 percent of the value of a "market portfolio" containing all stocks. And because these indexes capture the market factor well, the returns on stocks not included in them are nevertheless about as closely correlated with returns on these indexes as on more inclusive indexes.

The Value Line index, on the other hand, does not correspond directly to any portfolio of stocks because of its use of geometric averaging. Also, equal weighting of stock returns leads to much higher weight being placed on small firm returns than in the other indexes. Still, the VLA, containing over 1,700 companies, has the broadest coverage of the three broad market indexes. And because all stocks move with the market as a whole, any broad index will, too. Thus, the changes in the VLA are highly correlated on a day to day basis with the other indexes. However, divergences occur over longer time periods due to the effects of relatively heavier weighting of small stocks and geometric averaging. Table 6–2 shows correlations of these index changes over different time horizons.

Table 6–2.   Correlations in Percentage Changes among Major Stock Indexes over Various Horizons. 1 January 1980–31 December 1984.

			Correlation with		
Horizon	Index	Standard deviation	S&P	NYSE	Value Line
1 day	S&P	0.94	1.000	—	—
	NYSE	0.90	0.996	1.000	—
	Value Line	0.77	0.891	0.921	1.000
5 days	S&P	2.32	1.000	—	—
	NYSE	2.31	0.997	1.000	—
	Value Line	2.30	0.920	0.943	1.000
20 days	S&P	4.74	1.000	—	—
	NYSE	4.91	0.998	1.000	—
	Value Line	5.63	0.945	0.961	1.000
130 days	S&P	13.23	1.000	—	—
	NYSE	13.54	0.999	1.000	—
	Value Line	15.89	0.952	0.964	1.000

Note: Horizon is measured in trading days.

THE INDEX FUTURES CONTRACTS

This section will briefly discuss the stock index futures contracts based on the three broad market indexes: the S&P 500, the NYSE Composite, and the Value Line. The other narrower indexes, the S&P 100 and the MMI, are at present less likely to be of interest for hedging applications involving diversified institutional portfolios. Nevertheless, the broad principles of hedging, such as computation of hedge ratios, apply equally to all index futures.

Stock index futures represented a substantial innovation in futures trading for several reasons. Previous contracts were all based on a specific deliverable security or set of securities such as a particular Treasury bill, or a group of Treasury bonds with well-defined characteristics that could be delivered in fulfillment of the contract.

By contrast, physical delivery of stocks against a futures contract based on an index presented intractable difficulties. As we saw with the Value Line index, not every index corresponds to a portfolio of stocks. Moreover, it is not really feasible to construct a broad, market value weighted portfolio that is both of manageable size to be delivered and contains whole numbers of shares for all companies. And trying to do so approximately would entail enormous transactions costs.

This posed a hurdle to setting up an index futures market. What would connect the futures price to the cash market for stocks in order for effective hedging to be possible? The problem was resolved by the innovation of cash settlement. The underlying asset for a stock index futures contract is defined to be an amount of cash equal to $500 times the value of the index. At maturity, the final settlement price for the futures contract is set equal to the closing index on that date. This leads to one last mark to market from the previous day's settlement price, meaning one last cash transfer between long and short futures positions, and then the contract expires. There is no delivery of stock certificates, no uncertainty about which instrument will be the cheapest to deliver, and no possibility of corners or squeezes. The only requirement (which makes cash delivery suitable only for certain markets) is that the cash market price must be unambiguous and not subject to manipulation. Broad-based stock indexes satisfy these criteria very well.

Some of the important characteristics of the three major stock index futures contracts are shown in Table 6–3. As can be seen, they

Table 6–3.   Stock Index Futures Contracts Based on Broad Market Indexes.

	S&P	*NYSE*	*Value Line*
Exchange	Chicago Mercantile Exchange	New York Futures Exchange	Kansas City Board of Trade
Started trading	Apr. 1982	May 1982	Feb. 1982
Underlying index	Standard and Poor's 500	New York Stock Exchange Composite	Value Line Composite Average
Contract size	$500 × index	$500 × index	$500 × index
Contract months	March, June, Sept., Dec.	March, June, Sept., Dec.	March, June, Sept., Dec.
Delivery method	Cash Settlement	Cash Settlement	Cash Settlement
Minimum tick size	0.05	0.05	0.05
Price limits	None	None	None
Margin requirements Initial Maintenance	$6,000 $2,500	$3,500 $1,500	$6,500 $2,500

are all of similar design. In practice, the S&P 500 and the NYSE contracts are very similar, while the Value Line contract differs in a significant way because of the nature of its underlying index. There is some evidence that the fact that it is an equally weighted index may make it track the behavior of smaller stocks, such as those traded on the American Stock Exchange or over the counter better than the other indexes. This would tend to make it a better hedging vehicle for them, but lower liquidity due to its markedly lower trading volume might offset the advantage.

SYSTEMATIC RISK, INDEX RISK, AND BASIS RISK

The original idea behind a futures contract on a stock index was that since market risk is a major component of the total risk on all stocks and portfolios of stocks, a single futures contract based on "the market" could be useful to hedge the systematic risk of any stock position. But which index is "the market"? There are futures contracts based on three broad indexes to choose from, and others that might also be candidates. And how should one deal with contracts based on narrower indexes that might only contain large firms, or those in a certain industry?

The problem of defining the "true" market portfolio is not new in finance. Richard Roll, in a famous critique of the CAPM, raised this issue as a major problem with testing and using the model.[1] The theoretically correct answer shows that none of the indexes we use is even close to what the concept of the market portfolio really implies. The market portfolio should represent a value weighted cross-section of *all* assets in the economy. This would include, at a minimum, all stocks, bonds, and other corporate securities like warrants, preferred stock, and commercial paper; government securities, both federal and municipal; real estate and other real assets like gold; and so on. Naturally both domestic and international assets should be included.

Given the practical impossibility of looking only at the theoretically correct market portfolio, it still makes sense to make use of the fact that stock prices all tend to move up and down together in designing a futures contract to hedge these price fluctuations. It is just that there is no longer any necessarily best choice for an index to base the futures contract on. Different indexes will behave differently, and the choice of the appropriate contract for hedging a stock position will vary from case to case.

Thus, while most discussions of hedging with stock index futures center on "market" and "nonmarket" or "unsystematic" risk — as if these were unambiguously defined concepts — a more general approach, and terminology, would divide the random price fluctuations on a stock into the component that matches (is perfectly correlated with) movements in the index in question and the component that is independent. These two elements of risk might then be termed "index" risk and "nonindex" risk, with no implication about whether the index is broad or narrow, value weighted, equally weighted, or constructed in some other way, or indeed whether it is an index of stock prices at all (rather than, say, the Consumer Price Index).

---

1. Richard Roll, "A Critique of the Asset Pricing Theory's Tests: Part I...," *Journal of Financial Economics* (March 1977).

The measure of systematic risk is the beta coefficient, defined in equation (6.1) as the covariance between returns on the stock and returns on the market, divided by the variance of returns on the market. The same calculation can be used to measure index risk, bearing in mind that the betas of a given stock with respect to different indexes will be different. One simply replaces the return on the market by "the return on the index" in the equation. The index beta computed in this way has the same properties as the normal beta. In particular, the index beta of the index itself is 1.0, the index beta of a riskless security is zero, and the index beta of a portfolio is the value weighted average of the index betas of the component stocks.

In principle, the return on the market portfolio used in the regression (6.2) to estimate the market beta included dividends. Does this mean dividends must always be included when estimating index betas? The answer is no: If one includes dividends one derives the index beta with respect to the dividend inclusive index, and if they are not included, a different index beta is obtained because a different index is involved. (Practically, of course, since dividends are quite stable, these betas will normally be very similar.)

HEDGING STRATEGIES

The next part of this chapter will describe and illustrate a number of the most important risk management strategies that are possible using stock index futures. We will present a series of examples based on the portfolio of ten stocks shown in Table 6-4. This portfolio was selected from fairly large capitalization firms like those held in institutional portfolios, with some attempt to achieve diversification across industries. Quantities were chosen fairly randomly—in particular, returns experienced on the stocks were not a consideration in forming the portfolio. Our objective was not to duplicate a typical institutional investment portfolio but simply to pick a small collection of stocks that could be used to illustrate the strategies.

Designing a hedge requires knowledge of the correlation between returns on the portfolio being hedged and the futures contract. We will use the period from July 1982 through December 1983 to estimate the necessary parameters and then use them in hedging strategies during the first ten months of 1984. For the most part, we use monthly data. Although more sophisticated estimation techniques and daily

Table 6-4.   Sample Stock Portfolio.

Number of shares	Ticker symbol	Company name
5,000	ABC	American Broadcasting Company
10,000	AHP	American Home Products
5,000	BA	Boeing
10,000	EK	Eastman Kodak
10,000	GW	Gulf & Western
15,000	IBM	International Business Machines
5,000	PSY	Pillsbury
15,000	TX	Texaco
15,000*	WX	Westinghouse
10,000	Z	Woolworth

*In May 1984 Westinghouse split 2 for 1. The portfolio contains 15,000 new shares that were created from 7,500 old shares prior to the split.

data could be employed, in the examples we have preferred to use simple methods that can be applied relatively easily. The hedger must bear in mind that because economic relationships in the financial system are dynamic and continually changing, regardless of how accurately one estimates parameters from past data, they will never be exactly correct for the future. Often, simple methods that are more robust against estimation risk give superior performance over more elaborate procedures.

The set of risk-return combinations made available by selling futures to hedge a long position in stocks are described mathematically by equations (6.10) and (6.11):

$$E[R_h] = E[R_p] - hE[R_f] \qquad (6.10)$$

$$\sigma_h^2 = \sigma_p^2 + h^2\sigma_f^2 - 2h\rho_{pf}\sigma_f\sigma_p, \qquad (6.11)$$

where $E[R_h]$, $E[R_p]$, and $E[R_f]$ are the expected returns on the overall hedged position, the stock portfolio itself, and a long position in the futures contract, respectively. h is the hedge ratio, σ_h, σ_p, and σ_f are the standard deviations of return on the hedged position, the stock portfolio, and the futures contract, and ρ_{pf} is the correlation coefficient between the portfolio and the futures return.

Notice that the measures of risk and return have been changed somewhat from what was used in the earlier chapters. Since we no longer have the natural units of par equals one hundred to base price change calculations upon, it is more convenient to recast the hedging problem for stocks in terms of rates of return. This will slightly alter the procedures for computing and working with the hedge ratio.

For the purpose of illustration, in describing these hedge strategies we will concentrate primarily on the risk characteristics of the hedged position without taking explicit account of the effects of possible mispricing of the futures contract on hedge returns. How stock index futures should be priced in equilibrium and what strategies can be used to exploit mispricing will be discussed later. In actual application, the hedger must of course be aware of both risk and return, and recognize that certain strategies will become relatively costly or cheap as the futures price in the market trades at a premium or discount with respect to its theoretical value.

Estimating the Risk Parameters

The standard deviations and correlation in equation (6.11) are those relating to the rates of return on the portfolio being hedged and the futures contract to be used in the hedge. A number of variations are available in doing this estimation. We will describe one method that is internally consistent and relatively easy to apply.

We begin by computing the returns on a monthly basis using end of month prices for the stocks in the portfolio. The market value of the portfolio at the end of the month plus dividends for stocks going ex-dividend during the month is divided by the value at the end of the previous month—that is,

$$R_{pt} = \frac{V_t + D_t}{V_{t-1}} - 1, \qquad (6.12)$$

where R_{pt} is the portfolio return in month t, V_t is the total market value at the end of month t of all of the stock held, and D_t is the dividend. It is also possible to use returns without dividends, if that is more convenient, with only a small change in the results.

Unlike the price change, the "rate of return" on a futures contract is not a well-defined term since there is no initial investment in the usual sense. We will define it as the change in the futures price over the month divided by the initial value of the *cash* index.

$$R_{ft} = \frac{F_t - F_{t-1}}{I_{t-1}}, \qquad (6.13)$$

where R_{ft} is the return on the future, F_t is the futures price at the end of month t, and I_{t-1} is the level of the underlying stock index at the end of month $t-1$. This definition is consistent with our subsequent calculations. An alternative is to divide by the initial futures price. That definition of futures return would require another adjustment to be made in computing hedge ratios.

It is essential in computing futures returns to take proper account of futures expiration dates. We use the nearest to expiration futures contract, in all of these applications. Nearly all of the trading takes place in this contract so it is by far the most liquid. However, this means that it is necessary to roll over the hedge to the next contract every three months as the nearest one expires. Both in computing futures returns here and in our examples below, we assume the roll-over is done on the last day of the month prior to expiration. For example, the futures return for February is based on the change in the March futures price from 31 January to 28 February, while the futures return for March is based on the change in the June futures price from 28 February to 31 March. One must, of course, take care never to do any calculations that result in the returns being computed from the price difference between two different contracts.

The constant hedge ratio that minimizes the standard deviation of return on the hedged portfolio is equal to the covariance between the return on the portfolio and the return on the future, divided by the variance of return on the futures contract. This can also be computed as the correlation coefficient multiplied by the standard deviation of the portfolio divided by that of the future. That is,

$$h^* = \frac{\text{cov}[R_p, R_f]}{\text{var}[R_f]} = \rho_{pf} \frac{\sigma_p}{\sigma_f}. \qquad (6.14)$$

This is easily computed from estimates of these parameters, or it can be estimated directly by running a regression of the portfolio returns (as the dependent variable) on the futures returns (as the independent variable). A constant term should always be included in this regression.

Looking back to equation (6.1), one sees that h^* is essentially the "beta" of the portfolio with respect to the futures contract. Earlier discussion of hedging with index futures often suggested using the portfolio's beta with respect to the cash index as the appropriate hedge ratio. If this worked, it could save considerable effort in estimation, since estimated betas for stocks are readily available from many sources. Clearly, if $\text{cov}[R_p, R_I] = \text{cov}[R_p, R_f]$ and $\text{var}[R_I] = \text{var}[R_f]$, equations (6.1) and (6.14) would yield the same values. However, in practice these conditions typically do not hold. In general, futures are more volatile than the underlying index because of basis risk between the future and its index. The covariances need not be equal either. The result is that h^* may differ substantially from beta.[2]

Normally the effect of basis risk is to make h^* less than beta by an amount that is larger the shorter is the interval over which returns are calculated. For a hedge that is expected to last less than a month, the difference should not be ignored. On the other hand, for hedges of longer duration, basis risk becomes less important since the magnitude of possible changes in the basis become small relative to changes in the underlying index. In that case, h^* and beta will be approximately equal. Because of the effect of basis variations on futures returns, one should not use daily futures data to estimate risk parameters relating to hedges that will be held for significantly longer horizons.

Table 6–5 shows our estimates of the risk parameters for both the estimation period and the hedging period. Several features of the table are of interest. Notice first the effect of diversification in the fact that the correlation with the futures return is substantially higher for the overall portfolio than for any of the individual stocks. Index futures hedges for positions in individual stocks have been found for the most part to be fairly ineffective. This can be seen in the fact that the square of the correlation coefficient, which was discussed in Chapter 2 as a good measure of hedging effectiveness, is quite low for them. With correlation of 0.50 only 25 percent of the variance of returns is expected to be hedgeable.

A second useful comparison is between h^* and beta. During the estimation period and especially during the hedging period, they are quite close. In this case, with a one-month estimation interval, substituting beta for h^* gives a reasonable approximation, although they do differ substantially for certain individual stocks. Also notice that

2. See, for example, S. Figlewski, "Hedging Performance and Basis Risk in Stock Index Futures," *Journal of Finance* (July 1984).

Table 6-5. Hedging Parameters in Estimation Period and Hedging Period.

	Estimation period 7/1/82–12/31/83				Hedging period 1/2/84–11/1/84			
	Correlation	Standard deviation	h*	beta	Correlation	Standard deviation	h*	beta
ABC	0.411	0.071	0.64	1.00	0.660	0.077	1.15	1.17
AHP	0.375	0.057	0.47	0.62	0.382	0.049	0.42	0.39
BA	0.692	0.158	2.42	2.78	0.383	0.077	0.66	0.64
EK	0.433	0.069	0.66	0.72	−0.097	0.060	−0.13	−0.14
GW	0.576	0.116	1.48	1.62	0.646	0.073	1.07	1.01
IBM	0.535	0.056	0.66	0.75	0.796	0.054	0.97	0.94
PSY	0.522	0.077	0.89	1.12	0.345	0.046	0.36	0.32
TX	0.639	0.039	0.55	0.59	0.296	0.101	0.68	0.59
WX	0.594	0.080	1.06	1.03	0.897	0.098	1.98	1.95
Z	−0.007	0.114	−0.02	0.33	0.014	0.069	0.02	0.03
Total portfolio	0.809	0.039	0.71	0.84	0.931	0.038	0.79	0.76
Futures standard deviation		0.045				0.044		

beta is larger than h^* during the estimation period, as is usual, but that during the hedging period with only ten months of data, this relationship is reversed. In any case, one should see that for individual stocks the change in h^* or beta from one period to the next is larger than the difference between them within a period.

How much difference does our choice of futures contract make? We have chosen the S&P contract for this analysis, but the NYSE or Value Line could have been used. Table 6-6 shows the correlations with all three indexes during the estimation period and also presents figures for returns both with and without dividends. There is virtually no difference between the S&P and NYSE contracts in their ability to hedge this portfolio. Since these are all large companies, however, correlations with the Value Line contract are somewhat lower. But notice that again the differences between periods for a given contract are larger than differences between contracts. It is also apparent that whether dividends are included or excluded makes virtually no difference.

An alternative way to compute h^* is as a weighted average of the h^* parameters for the individual stocks in the portfolio. This makes revising the hedge ratio when portfolio composition changes much easier. The weight on h^* for stock i in forming the weighted average is just the market value of the shares held in stock i divided by the market value of the entire portfolio. Because of differences in relative performance of the individual stocks, there will typically be a slight difference between h^* calculated this way based on market value weights as of the end of the estimation period and h^* estimated from returns on the entire portfolio throughout the period, as we described above. In our case, for example, h^* from Table 6–5 was 0.71 while the weighted average h^* was 0.75.

Computing the Number of Contracts Needed

The hedge ratio h represents the dollar value of the amount of the index portfolio that one has contracted to *sell* in the futures market, divided by the dollar value of the portfolio one is hedging. (Algebraically, h is negative if one buys futures against a short position in the portfolio.)

$$h = \frac{\text{\$ Value of index portfolio sold in the futures market}}{\text{\$ Value of portfolio being hedged}}. \quad (6.15)$$

Table 6-6. Comparison of Correlations in Estimation Period 7/1/82–12/31/83.

	S&P		NYSE		Value Line	
	Dividend	No dividend	Dividend	No dividend	Dividend	No dividend
ABC	0.411	0.407	0.440	0.433	0.406	0.394
AHP	0.375	0.360	0.361	0.340	0.252	0.221
BA	0.692	0.696	0.722	0.725	0.780	0.783
EK	0.433	0.433	0.494	0.499	0.458	0.450
GW	0.576	0.576	0.609	0.611	0.603	0.607
IBM	0.535	0.506	0.496	0.462	0.377	0.340
PSY	0.522	0.513	0.528	0.519	0.455	0.450
TX	0.639	0.636	0.556	0.540	0.389	0.348
WX	0.594	0.603	0.626	0.633	0.690	0.699
Z	−0.007	−0.011	0.035	0.030	0.027	0.023
Portfolio	0.809	0.804	0.818	0.806	0.726	0.700
Portfolio in hedge period	0.931	0.952	0.930	0.950	0.887	0.902

In order to talk about the size of an index futures contract in the same terms used for other futures, it is useful to use the concept of an "index share." We define an index share as an amount of the underlying index portfolio whose value is equal to $1 times the index. For example, if the NYSE index is at 95.00, an NYSE index share represents $95.00 worth of the NYSE composite portfolio. One can also say that the price of an NYSE index share is $95.00. The broad stock index futures contracts are therefore based on 500 index shares of the underlying portfolio.

For example, assume that the S&P index is at 150.00 (i.e., the price of one index share is $150), and suppose the portfolio being hedged is currently worth $6,000,000. This means that the 500 index shares of the S&P index portfolio underlying one S&P futures contract have a current market value of $500 \times \$150 = \$75,000$. Selling twenty contracts would lead to a hedge ratio of

$$h = \frac{(20 \text{ contracts})(500 \times \$150.00)}{\$6,000,000}$$

$$= \frac{\$1,500,000}{\$6,000,000}$$

$$= 0.25.$$

To solve for the number of contracts that need to be traded in order to achieve a specified hedge ratio, this equation is rearranged. For example, suppose one wanted a hedge ratio of 0.80.

$$\text{Number of Contracts} = \frac{\text{Desired hedge ratio} \times \$ \text{Value of portfolio}}{\text{Number of index shares in futures contract} \times \text{Price of index share}}$$

$$= \frac{(0.80)(\$6,000,000)}{(500)(\$150.00)}$$

$$= 64. \tag{6.16}$$

So selling sixty-four S&P futures contracts would yield a hedge ratio of 0.80.

HEDGING EXAMPLES

We will now present a series of examples to illustrate how these concepts are applied in implementing major types of risk management strategies involving stock index futures.

Straight Hedge

Suppose the hedging objective is simply to minimize the risk of holding the stock portfolio displayed in Table 6–4. We will use the risk minimizing hedge ratio h^* estimated from monthly data over the period July 1982–December 1983 and compare the returns on the hedged position month by month during the first ten months of 1984 with the returns experienced by the portfolio held unhedged.

On 30 December 1983 the market value of the portfolio was $4,986,875 and the S&P 500 index was at 164.93. From Table 6–5 the appropriate hedge ratio h^* is 0.71. Plugging into equation (6.16) gives the number of S&P futures contracts to be sold.

$$\text{Number of contracts} = \frac{(0.71)(\$4,986,875)}{(500)(\$164.93)}$$

$$= 42.93.$$

Accordingly, forty-three March futures were sold. This futures position was held until 29 February. On that date it was assumed that the position was rolled over by buying the March futures back and selling forty-three June S&P contracts. A similar rollover to the next contract month was done again on 31 May and 31 August.

Table 6–7 shows the results of this strategy by month. The first ten months of 1984 were an exceptionally turbulent period for the stock market, with major drops in both February and May and an extraordinary runup during the month of August. On balance, equities did not perform terribly well during the year, and the monthly standard deviation of returns on the portfolio was 3.76 percent. Annualized (by multiplying by twelve in order to prevent August from dominating the result) mean returns were 8.29 percent with standard deviation of 45.08 percent. The futures hedge proved to be fairly (though

Table 6-7. Straight Hedge.

Month	Beginning of month portfolio value	Capital gain plus dividend	% Return on portfolio unhedged	Profit on futures hedge	% Return on hedged portfolio
JAN	4,986,875	−38,500	−0.77	38,700	0.00
FEB	4,938,750	−110,080	−2.23	179,525	1.41
MAR	4,789,070	14,430	0.30	−37,625	−0.48
APR	4,801,250	58,445	1.22	−7,525	1.06
MAY	4,849,695	−160,720	−3.31	227,900	1.39
JUN	4,649,375	14,125	0.30	−33,325	−0.41
JUL	4,661,250	63,750	1.37	55,900	2.57
AUG	4,715,000	493,725	10.47	−325,725	3.56
SEPT	5,166,875	−62,125	−1.20	2,150	1.16
OCT	5,102,500	39,200	0.77	32,250	1.40
Mean			0.69		0.93
Standard deviation			3.76		1.46
Beta			0.76		0.07
Annualized:					
Mean			8.29		11.19
Standard deviation			45.08		17.58

not completely) effective at moderating the swing in returns. The standard deviation was cut by over 60 percent to an annualized figure of 17.58 percent. Note also that the beta of the position dropped from 0.76 to 0.07, so that market risk was almost completely hedged. Along with this went an increase in mean return over the period. Thus the hedge performed very well.

Naturally, one should not expect both a drop in risk *and* an increase in return under normal circumstances. If the stock market had had a good year and substantially outperformed riskless securities, the excess returns would have been largely given up in a hedged position. The important property of a hedge is that it improves performance when the market does not do well, as happened in 1984.

Market Timing

One of the primary strategies of active portfolio managers is market timing, increasing their portfolio's equity exposure by raising its beta when the stock market is expected to go up and reducing exposure when expectations are less favorable. Index futures greatly facilitate changing a portfolio's beta because they can be bought or sold quickly, in quantity, and with low transactions costs. This should make trading stock index futures the method of choice for most market timing.

During the estimation period, our portfolio's beta was 0.84. Suppose as a market timing strategy we had wanted to lower its beta to 0.50 at the end of April and raise it to 1.0 at the end of July. Let us examine the results over the six-month period through the end of October.

30 April: Portfolio value $4,849,695
S&P index 160.05

To reduce the portfolio's beta from 0.84 to 0.50, set the hedge ratio to 0.34.

$$\text{Number of contracts} = \frac{(0.34)(\$4,849,695)}{(500)(\$160.05)}$$

$$= 20.6.$$

Sell twenty-one June S&P 500 futures (roll over on 31 May).

31 July: Portfolio value = \$4,715,000
S&P index = 150.66

Cover the short position in futures and raise the portfolio beta from 0.84 to 1.00 by buying futures with a hedge ratio of 0.16.

$$\text{Number of contracts to buy} = \frac{(0.16)(\$4,715,000)}{(500)(\$150.66)}$$

$$= 10.0.$$

Buy ten September S&P 500 futures (roll over on 31 August).

Result:

	Portfolio Return			Futures Profit	Total Position
	Capital Gain	Dividend	Total		
May–July	−134,690	51,800	−82,845	122,325	39,480
Aug.–Oct.	392,500	78,300	470,800	67,750	538,550
May–Oct.	257,805	130,150	387,955	190,075	578,030

The result of this successful market timing strategy was that the six-month return on the portfolio was increased by \$190,075 over a buy and hold strategy, which translates to an extra 11.9 percent over the period (25.3 percent annualized). Of course, the original timing decisions about how and when to change the portfolio's market exposure had to be correct. If the wrong decisions had been made, for example raising the beta in April and lowering it in July, the outcome would have been much different.

What would the transactions costs of this strategy have been? Suppose direct costs in the form of brokerage commissions amounted to \$25 per contract round trip. Since thirty-one contracts were traded and each was rolled over once, there was a total of sixty-two round-trip commissions, for \$1,550. To this would have to be added the indirect trading cost of a one-tick bid-ask spread. This amounts to another \$25 per round trip, making the total transactions cost, conservatively estimated, \$3,100. This is obviously much less than it would have cost to alter the portfolio's beta in the same way by trading the stocks themselves.

Stock Selection

The two ways that active portfolio managers attempt to achieve higher returns than the market on average are through market timing and stock selection. We have just shown how a portfolio's overall market exposure can be adjusted using stock index futures. Stock selection consists of trying to buy stocks that individually will outperform the market and to avoid stocks that will underperform. The excess return over the expected return implied by the CAPM in equation (6.3) is known as a stock's "alpha." Successful stock selection, then, consists of buying stocks with positive alphas and selling, or at least avoiding, stocks with negative alphas.

In addition to the basic problem of predicting which stocks will have positive alphas, stock selection involves another problem in that every stock contains market risk. While a well chosen portfolio may beat the market significantly with an alpha of 2 percent, the overall return could still be unsatisfactory if the market was down. Moreover, there may be conflicts when a stock with an expected high alpha also has a high beta, which would lead to an undesirable increase in market exposure if it is added to a portfolio.

By allowing market risk to be managed independently of portfolio composition, a stock index futures hedge can allow a portfolio manager to amplify the effect of his stock picking ability without increasing the market risk of his portfolio.

Over the first ten months of 1984, as it turned out, our example portfolio outperformed the S&P 500.

Total return on S&P 500 portfolio = 4.30%
Total return on our portfolio   = 6.49%
Return on 1-month Treasury bills   = 7.97%.

Plugging these numbers into the CAPM to find our portfolio's realized alpha over this period gives:

Predicted return = riskless return
            + beta × (market return–riskless return)
         = 7.97 + 0.84 (4.30 − 7.97)
         = 4.89%.

$$\text{Alpha} = \text{actual return–predicted return}$$
$$= 6.49 - 4.89$$
$$= 1.60\%.$$

Suppose the portfolio manager's objective had been to hold the market exposure of the portfolio down to a level equivalent to 40 percent invested in the stock market and 60 percent invested in cash (i.e., a beta of 0.40). One way to do this would be to put the fraction $0.40/0.84 = 48$ percent of the funds into the stock portfolio and hold the remaining 52 percent in one month Treasury bills. The return on the resulting portfolio would have been

$$\text{Return on stock/bill portfolio} = (0.48)(6.49\%) + (0.52)(7.97\%)$$
$$= 7.27\%.$$

Since this portfolio had only forty-eight percent of the funds invested in stocks its alpha would have been forty-eight percent of the stock portfolio's alpha, or 0.77 percent. Another way to lower the beta is by placing all of the funds in stocks and selling futures to bring the beta down to the target level. The hedge ratio required to accomplish this is $h = 0.84 - 0.40 = 0.44$.

Initial value of portfolio	$4,986,875
Initial level of S&P index	164.93

$$\text{Number of contracts} = \frac{(0.44)(\$4,986,875)}{(500)(\$164.93)}$$
$$= 26.71.$$

Therefore twenty-seven S&P futures contracts were sold.

Total return over 10 months to futures hedge $= \$83,025$

$$\text{Return on hedged position} = 6.49\% + \frac{83,025}{4,986,875}$$
$$= 8.15\%.$$

This strategy allowed the alpha of 1.60 percent to be earned on the entire investment while holding the market risk to the target level. The result was a portfolio that outperformed the S&P 500,

Treasury bills, and the alternative investment strategy that gave the same beta.

Flexibility in Liquidating a Portfolio

A major problem is faced by a portfolio manager when he wants to liquidate positions in less liquid securities. Institutional sized blocks of any but the most broadly traded issues take time and care to be disposed of without driving prices down significantly. During the process of liquidation, the portfolio is exposed to market movements. This risk exposure can be hedged by selling stock index futures, allowing the manager more time to wait for attractive selling opportunities to develop for the individual stocks. As the portfolio liquidation proceeds, the short futures contracts are bought back so as to keep the remaining holdings correctly hedged. One should recognize also, that as the number of issues still held is reduced, the portfolio becomes less diversified. Basis risk is likely to become more serious and the hedge will become less effective.

To illustrate one way such a liquidation might be managed with an index futures hedge, suppose that at the end of March 1984 the decision was made to sell out our stock portfolio in the following way. The price of each stock would be monitored daily and it would be sold whenever its price closed 5 percent or more above the 30 March level. Stocks that had not been sold by 31 May would be liquidated at the closing prices on that date. During the period a futures hedge would be maintained to minimize the market risk on the remaining stocks.

Table 6–8 gives the 30 March prices and total dollar investments in the ten stocks, and the hedge ratio and number of futures contracts assigned to each:

The strategy we described led to the transactions outlined in Table 6–9. By following this liquidation strategy, five of the ten stocks were sold for 5 percent or more above their 30 March prices, and the futures hedge protected the value of the remaining stocks during a period in which the market was down overall. In addition, dividends were received during the liquidation period on seven of the stocks. Let us compare the results with what would have been obtained under the alternative strategies of selling all of the stocks on 30 March or holding all of them until 30 May, with or without a futures hedge.

Table 6-8.   Hedge Ratios for Individual Stocks.

		March 30 values		
Stock	*Price*	*Value of holding*	*h**	*Number of contracts*
ABC	58½	292,500	0.64	2.4
AHP	52⅝	526,250	0.47	3.1
BA	38⅛	190,625	2.42	5.8
EK	63⅝	318,125	0.66	2.6
GW	31¾	317,500	1.48	5.9
IBM	114	1,710,000	0.66	14.2
PSY	37⅝	188,125	0.89	2.1
TX	39½	592,500	0.55	4.1
WX	22⅜	335,625	1.06	4.5
Z	33	330,000	−0.02	−0.1
Total		4,801,250		44.6

Notes: The S&P index on 30 March was 159.18.
Westinghouse split 2 for 1 in May. The price is quoted in terms of new shares.

Strategy	*Proceeds of Cash Market Transactions*	*Proceeds of Futures Transactions*	*Total Proceeds*
Sell all stocks on 30 March	$4,801,250	—	$4,801,250
Sell all stocks on 31 May	$4,649,375	—	$4,649,375
Hedge whole portfolio on 30 March (45 futures contracts sold). Liquidate position on 31 May	$4,649,375	$230,625	$4,880,000
Gradual liquidation as described in the example	$4,754,062	$152,250	$4,906,312

Thus the gradual liquidation strategy made possible by the stock index futures hedge proved to be the best of the four. Indeed, a factor

Table 6-9. Liquidation of Portfolio.

| | Stocks | | | Futures | | |
Date	Transaction	Price	Value	Transaction	Price	Profit
Mar 30				sell 45 June futures	161.05	—
Apr 16	sell 10,000 GW	33⅞	338,750	buy 6 futures	160.40	1,950
Apr 24	sell 5,000 PSY	40	200,000	buy 2 futures	159.35	1,700
Apr 26	sell 15,000 WX	23 9/16	353,438	buy 5 futures	161.15	−250
Apr 27	sell 10,000 AHP	55⅜	553,750	buy 3 futures	160.90	225
May 3	sell 10,000 Z	35	350,000			
May 31	sell 5,000 ABC	57	285,000	buy 29 futures	150.80	148,625
May 31	sell 5,000 BA	39	195,000			
May 31	sell 5,000 EK	66¼	331,250			
May 31	sell 15,000 IBM	107¾	1,616,250			
May 31	sell 15,000 TX	35⅜	530,000			
	Total		4,754,062			152,250

we have neglected in this calculation – interest that would have been earned by reinvesting the earlier cash flows from the first and last strategies – would have improved its relative performance further. The important point is that an index futures hedge increases a portfolio manager's options in liquidating an equity position.

The reader will have noticed that the strategy we illustrated here is not exactly the one discussed at first. The stocks in the example portfolio are all actively traded issues, and the problems of disposing of these relatively small positions would not be serious. The success of this liquidation program came from the fact that it exploited the price volatility of the stocks over the liquidation period. While this is a legitimate trading strategy, using our portfolio we were not able to demonstrate the true value of this sort of a hedge in liquidating large holdings of thinly traded issues. In that case the hedge allows the manager time to uncover a willing buyer where there might not be one immediately available at the outset.

Anticipatory Hedge

The hedge strategies we have discussed so far mostly involved selling index futures to protect an existing portfolio investment against a possible drop in stock prices. There are times, however, when the problem is not that stocks might drop but rather that they might go up too soon. It may happen, for example, that a portfolio manager anticipates an inflow of cash in the near future and believes that stocks present a good investment opportunity at current levels. But if the market rallies before the funds are received, the opportunity will be missed. What he would like to do is lock in current stock prices for an investment that will only be made in the future. This can be done by buying stock index futures today and selling them when funds are actually invested in stocks, a strategy known as an "anticipatory hedge" because it is a hedge not of an existing cash market position but one that is *anticipated* to develop.

To illustrate the anticipatory hedge, suppose that on 29 June funds are available to purchase only one-third of our stock portfolio but that cash inflows are expected that will permit another third to be purchased at the end of July and the last third at the end of August. The concern is that if the market were to rally over the summer, the total cost of the investment would increase. To protect against this possibility, S&P futures will be bought against two-thirds of the anticipated investment. These will be sold when the actual stocks are purchased on 31 July and 28 August.

29 June: Value of total portfolio $4,661,250
Futures will be purchased against 2/3 $3,107,500
S&P index   153.18
Minimum risk h^* 0.71

$$\text{Number of contracts} = \frac{(0.71)(3,107,500)}{(153.18)(500)}$$

$$= 28.8.$$

Buy twenty-nine September S&P futures contracts in place of two-thirds of the portfolio.

Date	Stock Transactions	Cost
29 June	Buy one-third of portfolio	$1,553,750
31 July	Buy one-third of portfolio	$1,571,667
28 August	Buy one-third of portfolio	$1,722,292
	Total cost	$4,847,708

Date	Futures Transactions	Price	Profit on Futures
29 June	Buy 29 SEP futures	154.85	
31 July	Sell 15 SEP futures	152.25	$ − 19,500
28 August	Sell 14 SEP futures	167.40	$ 106,050
	Total profit on futures hedge		$ 86,550.

Total cost increase of portfolio over 29 June value = $186,458.

Cost saving due to anticipatory hedge = $86,550 or 1.79%.

These have been a few of the most important types of hedges that are of interest to an institutional investor in equities. Others may be useful in particular cases. What index futures really offer is flexibility in managing stock portfolios. The applications of this flexibility are almost unlimited.

THE PRICE RELATIONSHIP BETWEEN INDEX
FUTURES AND THE UNDERLYING INDEX

Having shown how stock index futures can be used in a variety of strategies to alter portfolio risk, we will now turn to the pricing of the index futures contract. The impact of a stock index futures hedge on the rate of return on a position in stocks will depend on how the futures are priced relative to the current level of the underlying index. Like futures on fixed income securities, stock index futures prices should be related to the current price in the cash market by a cost of carry relationship. Otherwise an arbitrage opportunity exists. However, index futures differ from other financial futures because the arbitrage trade is difficult to do. Practically, this results in fairly wide deviations of actual futures prices from the cost of carry levels. This, in turn, means that the cost of hedging may vary considerably from time to time.

We will first outline the cost of carry pricing relation for stock index futures. This will apply to any index contract that is based on the value of a portfolio of stocks, whether it is market value weighted, equally weighted, or constructed in some other way. It does not directly apply to the Value Line contract because geometric averaging precludes duplicating the index with a portfolio of stocks.

The cost of carry pricing relation for a given stock index futures contract will depend on the current level of the index, the riskless interest rate, and the dividend payout on the index portfolio. Consider the investment strategy of buying stocks to duplicate the underlying index portfolio, selling the index futures contract against the position so that it is completely hedged, and holding until the futures expire. For example, one could invest in the NYSE composite index portfolio, a value weighted cross-section of all of the stocks traded on the New York Stock Exchange. If the index stood currently at some level I_0 an investment of, say, $50,000 times I_0 in this portfolio could be hedged exactly by selling one hundred NYSE index futures contracts.

The initial cost per index share of this investment strategy is just I_0, the initial level of the index. At expiration of the futures contracts, date T, the value of the stock portfolio will be I_T while the futures hedge will return $F_0 - I_T$ per index share hedged. This is the difference between the futures price at the outset and at date T, with the latter being equal by definition to the index on that date. Thus the hedge will have locked in a capital gain of $F_0 - I_0$ on the portfolio. During the holding period there will also be dividends paid out regularly by the stocks. Let $D(T)$ denote the dividend payout on date t per index share. Since the total dividend on a large portfolio is highly predictable, the entire cash flow on the hedged position over the holding period is essentially riskless. This means that the cost of the strategy at the outset should be just equal to the discounted present value of the known future cash flows, using the riskless interest rate applying to each future date as the appropriate discount rate. Let $PV(t)$ refer to the present value of \$1 to be paid at date t. We then have

$$I_0 = PV(T)F_0 + \sum_{t=1}^{T} PV(t)D(t). \qquad (6.17)$$

The initial cost is the present value of the future cash flows. Solving for the futures price that makes this true yields

$$F_0 = \frac{1}{PV(T)} \left[I_0 - \sum_{t=1}^{T} PV(t)D(t) \right]. \qquad (6.18)$$

Example: Take the simplified case of a three-month future on an index that only has one dividend payout, occurring two months in the future. Assume the initial level of the index is 90.00, the annual riskless interest rate is constant and equal to 12 percent, and the dividend per index share is \$1.00. Then,

$$PV(2) = 1/[1 + (2/12).12] = 1/1.02$$
$$PV(3) = 1/[1 + (3/12).12] = 1/1.03$$
$$F_0 = \frac{1}{PV(3)} [90.00 - PV(2)1.00]$$
$$= (1.03)(90.00 - 0.98)$$
$$F_0 = 91.69.$$

The index future in this case should be at 91.69. (Note that for ease of exposition we use a simple interest calculation in discounting.)

Unfortunately for those who need to calculate theoretical prices for stock index futures, dividend streams on actual stock indexes resemble a continuous daily payout more than they do the single payment assumed in the example. But, they are more complicated. First, payouts tend to be rather "lumpy," with relatively large values concentrated at certain points toward the middle of the calendar quarter and extra payouts at year end. Also, because stocks go ex-dividend some weeks before the dividend is actually paid, exact calculation should include only dividends for stocks that have ex-dividend dates after the initial date and before futures maturity, but the discounting should be from the date of payment. However, in most cases, a reasonable approximation for nearby futures is simply to assume that the entire dividend flow for the holding period occurs as a lump sum at the halfway point between today and expiration.

Prices on stock index futures should be driven by arbitrage forces toward the cost of carry level. However, unlike the case of futures on fixed income securities, the arbitrage between stocks and stock index futures is not easy. The transactions costs and execution delays in assembling the Standard and Poor's 500 portfolio in order to trade it against S&P futures are a formidable obstacle to arbitrage. This means deviations can arise and persist over relatively long periods, translating into both basis risk and periods during which hedging is relatively costly or relatively cheap. In a study of this phenomenon in S&P 500 futures, it was found that from June 1982 through September 1983 the contract nearest to expiration was overpriced on average by 0.21 (relative to an index value in the range of 100–170) with a standard deviation of 1.00.[3] The second contract from expiration was underpriced by 0.08 on average with a standard deviation of 1.43. In other words, the futures price was quite close to the theoretical value on average, but there were fairly wide deviations over time.

We have calculated the theoretical prices for the futures contracts used in the hedging examples above. The one-month Treasury bill rate was taken as the riskless interest rate. The difficult part is computing the present value of the stream of dividends to be paid up to the futures expiration date, expressed in terms of the index. This calculation can actually be rather cumbersome, since it is necessary to project the dividends to be paid on each stock in the index up to the futures expiration, cumulate them for each date using the appropriate portfolio weight, convert these daily totals into the same basis as the index, and then discount each element of the resulting series back to the initial date.

Calculating the Dividend Yield on a Stock Index (A)

The following procedure is one way to compute the present value of dividends to be paid on an index from a specified date $(t = 0)$ up to expiration of a futures contract $(t = T)$:

---

3. S. Figlewski, "Hedging Performance and Basis Risk in Stock Index Futures," *Journal of Finance* (July 1984).

1. Include all dividends for stocks going ex-dividend within the time period. Compute the total to be paid by all stocks in the index by day.

$$TD_t = \sum_{i=1}^{N} TD_{it} S_i,$$

where TD_t is the total number of dollars to be paid by stocks going ex-dividend on date t, TD_{it} is the dividend to be paid per share for stock i (0 if the stock does not go ex-dividend on date t), and S_i is the number of shares outstanding for stock i.

2. To convert the series of total dividends to the same basis as the index compute a conversion factor, K. Since it only changes when the composition of the index changes this need only be done once (or once in a while). For an arbitrarily chosen date, divide the level of the index on that day by the total value of the index portfolio.

$$K = I_0 \left/ \sum_{i=1}^{N} S_i P_{i0}, \right.$$

where P_{i0} is the price of stock i on the chosen date and I_0 is the level of the index. Multiply each total dividend figure in the series by K to express it in terms of the index:

$$D(t) = KTD_t.$$

The resulting $D(t)$ series can then be plugged into equation (6.18). Fortunately, a number of data services provide estimates of the dividend payout by day for the major indexes. When dividend series can be obtained from a data service, some or all of the steps can be eliminated. For example, we used a series of total dividends paid on the S&P index from the Interactive Data Corporation, thus eliminating step one. Our K factor, computed from the total market value of all S&P stocks on 1 June 1982, was 111.68/$792,593,400,000.

Theoretical S&P Futures Prices

Table 6–10 shows the theoretical futures prices at the beginning of each of the first ten months of 1984. In comparing the theoretical values to the actual prices in the market, we find that market prices were higher in every month. While this might appear to be evidence that there is something missing in the theory and that futures prices will, for some reason, always be priced higher than their cost of carry values, in fact it reverses the relationship that held with some consis-

Table 6-10. Theoretical Futures Prices.

Month	Index	Contract month	Present value of $1 at expiration	Present value of dividends	Theoretical futures price	Actual futures price	% Over valuation	Annualized return to arbitrage
JAN	164.93	MAR	0.980	1.781	166.45	167.30	0.52	2.13
FEB	163.41	MAR	0.986	1.458	164.18	165.50	0.81	5.13
MAR	157.06	JUN	0.973	2.425	158.97	159.30	0.21	0.64
APR	159.18	JUN	0.978	1.885	160.86	161.05	0.12	0.50
MAY	160.05	JUN	0.985	1.619	160.74	161.40	0.41	2.56
JUN	150.55	SEP	0.973	2.334	152.32	153.30	0.65	1.93
JUL	153.18	SEP	0.979	1.752	154.59	154.85	0.17	0.66
AUG	150.66	SEP	0.983	1.438	151.69	152.25	0.37	2.14
SEP	166.68	DEC	0.972	2.423	168.98	170.20	0.73	2.40
OCT	166.10	DEC	0.978	1.979	167.84	170.10	1.36	6.00

Note: Present values are computed using the one-month Treasury bill rate for discounting.

tency in previous years. When stock index futures first began trading in 1982, the futures price was regularly too low, even trading at a discount to the cash index on occasion.[4] If futures sell at a premium it tends to make short hedging relatively more attractive and long hedging more costly. Since the basis, by definition, must go to zero at expiration, the higher the future is relative to the cash index, the higher should be the return on a position that is long stock and short futures. However, an important caveat is that in order to realize this overpricing as a profit, the future must be priced correctly when the short sale is covered. By definition, this can be done at expiration when the final futures price is set equal to the cash index, but there is no guarantee of it at any point before then. This means that overpricing of the future will not necessarily increase the return on a short hedge that is closed out early or rolled over to a later contract month. For example, although the futures price at the start of January was eighty-five points above its theoretical level, the change in the basis during the month actually caused a short hedge to lose value as overvaluation increased to 122 points by the beginning of February.

Mispricing of stock index futures appears to be largely related to expectations. Because of the difficulty of arbitraging between the cash and futures markets, bullish or bearish expectations among futures traders can drive the price relatively far away from its theoretical value. And because changes in expectations, like the direction of price movement in the market, are very hard to forecast with accuracy, fluctuations in the amount of mispricing are largely unpredictable.

One additional factor that compounds the problem is that to the extent that changes in the basis are driven by expectations, the basis will tend to move unfavorably to what most potential hedgers would like to be doing. For example, when the outlook for stocks is poor, portfolio managers would like to reduce market exposure by selling index futures. But because of the widespread bearish sentiment, it is likely that futures will be priced relatively low, making a short hedge more costly. Similarly, when everyone believes the market is going up, index futures will tend to sell at a premium and going long in the futures market becomes more expensive.

The relatively wide fluctuations in the basis give rise to profitable arbitrage, or more properly quasi-arbitrage, strategies. The most direct

---

4. S. Figlewski, "Explaining the Early Discounts on Stock Index Futures...," *Financial Analysts Journal* (Jul-Aug 1984).

possibilities would involve trading between the future and an investment portfolio designed to duplicate the index underlying the futures contract. At this time substantial sums are being held in passive portfolios indexed to the S&P 500. The S&P future allows a fund manager to lock in a future capital value for such a portfolio. When the future sells below its theoretical value, it is cheaper to "buy the S&P portfolio in the futures market," by placing funds in money market securities and going long futures, than it is to buy the stocks themselves. At expiration of the futures contracts, the interest received plus the profit (or loss) on the futures hedge will more than offset the dividends and capital gain (or loss) that would have been received on the portfolio of stocks. If the future is overpriced, it becomes attractive to place funds that would otherwise be held in cash into the S&P portfolio and sell futures against it. At expiration the capital gain locked in by the short hedge plus the dividends received on the portfolio will produce a total return that is riskless and higher than that offered by money market securities.

The last column in Table 6-10 shows the annualized extra return that such an arbitrage strategy would have yielded if it had been implemented at the opening prices for each month in 1984 (actually, at the last closing prices of the previous month.) That is, no attempt was made to pick the dates on which such an arbitrage would have been most profitable. Still, at times highly attractive opportunities existed. In practice, some institutional investors have been reported to have earned annual alpha's greater than 5 percent on funds that were essentially invested passively in an S&P index fund by engaging in this type of arbitrage.

7 MANAGING A POSITION

The previous chapters have dealt with the theoretical and practical aspects of designing a hedge strategy with financial futures. In this chapter we will discuss the details of trading a hedged position, including initiating a hedging program, putting on a hedge, carrying a position, rolling over to later expiration months, and making and taking delivery.

CHOOSING A FUTURES COMMISSION MERCHANT

One of the most important decisions in initiating a hedging program is to choose the futures commission merchant (FCM) that will execute the trades. Unless the hedger plans to buy exchange seats, it is necessary to trade through an FCM, which is either a member of the clearing house or is affiliated with a clearing member. Orders will be given to the FCM and executed on the floor of the exchange by the FCM's floor brokers. There are several important criteria to consider in choosing an FCM to trade through.

One primary consideration is commissions. At this time, commissions are negotiable on all futures exchanges. Commissions are charged on a round-trip basis, payable when the position is closed out. Retail commissions from a full-service broker can run as high as $100 per contract, while discount brokers routinely charge around $25. Exchange members typically pay commissions of only $2 to $3 per contract if they are not members of the clearing house, and even less if they are. This suggests that a large institution trading in volume might be able to negotiate commission rates in the range of $10 to $20 without too much difficulty if additional services, like extensive market research, are not required.

A second major consideration is execution. Given the relatively low commissions for futures trading and the nature of trading in a futures pit, the difference between good and bad execution of orders can make a significant difference in profitability in a hedging program. For example, one tick, the smallest allowable price change, is $25 for a stock index or Treasury bill contract and $31.25 for a Treasury note or bond contract. That means that a good execution that gains one tick on a trade might easily reduce the total transactions cost by 50 percent or more. Getting the best possible execution is especially important when a large number of contracts must be traded at one time in a market with limited liquidity.

One reason that the quality of execution can differ among FCM's is that there is no time priority in the pit regarding the execution of limit orders. Unlike the stock market, where orders placed on the specialist's book are executed in order of arrival, in a futures pit all orders at a given price are on the same footing, regardless of when they may have arrived and regardless of whether they represent public orders from an off-the-floor customer or the bids and offers of professional scalpers. For that reason, a floor broker who is quick and aggressive may be able to achieve substantially better execution than another who is not so adept.

A second potential execution problem is that floor brokers are allowed to execute public orders at the same time as they are trading for their own account in the same market. This naturally creates the possibility of conflicts of interest. If the opportunity to trade at a favorable price arises, the broker may want to trade for himself in preference to obtaining a good execution for his customer. For both of these reasons, execution can differ substantially from one firm to another. If dual trading by floor brokers is a concern, an institution might prefer to choose an FCM that does not allow its floor brokers to trade on their own account.

In addition to executing trades, an FCM can offer advice and assistance in setting up a hedging program, market research, ideas for different strategies, accounting and other services, and so on. Especially when a firm is first starting up a hedging program, the assistance of an experienced FCM may be particularly valuable. Such services add another dimension to the problem of choosing the best FCM.

Finally, one very important criterion is capital adequacy. While transactions cleared through the clearing house are protected against default by a customer of another clearing member or by the clearing member firm itself, a public customer should be aware that in many cases the exchange guarantee does not protect it against default by its *own* FCM or clearing firm. One reason for this is that most clearing houses require margin deposits from the clearing firms only on a net basis. That is, the clearing firm adds up all of the long positions held by its customers and all of the short positions, then deposits margin with the clearing house only on the overall *net* long or short position. For instance, a firm carrying accounts with an aggregate long position of one hundred contracts and an aggregate short position of ninety-five contracts would only be required to deposit margin for the five contracts it is net long with the clearing house. The customer margin deposits for the rest would simply be held by the FCM. (The Chicago Mercantile Exchange is the only major exchange requiring margin deposits on a gross basis. In this case, that would mean margin on 195 contracts would be required from the FCM.)

The problem with this system is that in the case of a major default — let us say by a customer holding fifty contracts short — any shortfall in the variation margin to be paid to fifty of the long contracts would have to be made up out of the FCM's own capital. If that were to prove inadequate, the position of the longs would be jeopardized. On 19 March 1985, gold futures on the COMEX experienced a record price advance that led to a default by a group of investors who had written (i.e., sold short) some 12,000 gold call option contracts. This precipitated the failure of their clearing firm, in which the other customers of the firm lost funds they had on deposit. As long as margining on a net basis is allowed, it is only prudent for a customer to take the capitalization of the FCM into account in deciding whom to do business with.

MARGINS

One of the most important aspects of futures trading is complying with margin requirements. The margining system used for futures is an integral part of the futures business, and it is completely different from that used for stocks or other securities. Even the meaning of the word margin is different for futures. Stock margin represents a downpayment on a stock purchase, with the remainder being borrowed through the broker. Thus buying $1 million of stock on 50 percent margin involves a margin deposit with the brokerage firm of $500,000 and a loan of $500,000. Initial margin on futures contracts, by contrast, is simply a good-faith deposit to guarantee performance in the future on the commitment that is entered into when the trade is initiated. There is no loan involved, and both the buyer and seller must post the same margin, since both are equally bound to perform on their contracts. Since futures margin is essentially collateral rather than a downpayment on an asset purchase, the initial margin requirement set by the exchange is held as low as possible, consistent with the need to guarantee the financial integrity of the contracts. Moreover, margin need not be posted in cash. Other securities, typically Treasury bills, can be used. Large traders and financial institutions may be able to post margin in the form of a bank letter of credit, thus eliminating the need to have investment funds tied up in margin deposits at all. While the exchanges set minimum margin requirements, clearing firms and FCMs can require margin deposits greater than the minimum. It is also up to the FCM to determine the terms under which initial margin in the form of interest bearing securities will be accepted.

Since the margin deposit is meant only to serve as a performance bond, the required margin level may be revised from time to time, as recent futures price volatility and other measures of risk change. Also, certain lower risk positions may be allowed more favorable margin treatment. In particular, required margin on futures contracts used in a bona fide hedge is frequently lower than on a "naked" position. The same is true of margin on a spread (in which a long position in one contract month offsets a short position in a different month). What defines a bona fide hedge can vary from market to market. In general the issue is determined by the FCM, and the definition is usually broad enough to include all legitimate hedging applications for an institutional investor.

Table 7–1 shows the current margin requirements for the major financial futures contracts as of 29 May 1985. These are subject to change, and it is necessary to determine the margin requirements in force at the time a hedge transaction is entered into.

A margin requirement actually consists of two levels, initial margin and maintenance margin. Initial margin, which we have been discussing so far, must be on deposit in order to open a futures position.

Table 7–1. Margin Requirements for Financial Futures (as of 29 May 1985).

	Initial	Maintenance	Hedge initial	Hedge maintenance
Short-term rates				
Treasury Bills	1,000	700	1,000	700
Eurodollar Deposits	1,000	700	1,000	700
Domestic CD's	1,000	700	1,000	700
Intermediate and Long-term debt				
Treasury Notes	1,750	1,500	1,500	1,500
Treasury Bonds	1,750	1,500	1,500	1,500
Stock indexes				
S&P 500	6,000	2,500	3,000	2,500
NYSE	3,500	1,500	1,500	1,200
Value Line	6,500	2,000	2,500	1,500
Contract sizes	Short-term	— $1,000,000 principal value		
	Debt	— $100,000 face value, 8% coupon		
	Stock indexes	— $500 × index		

Once a position has been established, it is marked to market every day (or, in rare cases, more frequently), and the day's paper profits and losses are transferred from the losing accounts to the winning accounts. This must be done in cash, so when the initial margin is posted in the form of securities or a letter of credit, it will be necessary either to liquidate a portion of the securities or to deposit additional cash in the account if a loss on a futures position occurs. As losses accrue (assuming no additional funds are deposited to cover them) the margin deposit diminishes. When it falls to the "maintenance margin" level, a margin call will be issued, which will require that additional margin be deposited to bring the total back up to the initial level. These funds must typically be deposited within twenty-four or forty-eight hours, or else the FCM can liquidate the customer's position in order to protect itself against the possibility of further losses that might lead to a default.

A hedger must monitor the margin position at all times in order to be prepared to meet margin calls as they occur. This requires planning and preparation, as in many cases the position being hedged will not generate cash flow before it is liquidated. Although the change in value of the cash position will offset losses on the futures contracts, the funds needed to meet variation margin calls must be obtained from another source. A well-designed hedging program will provide for a pool of liquid funds that can be used to meet margin calls as they occur. Otherwise, a hedged position might have to be liquidated at an unfavorable time in order to avoid the risk of cash outflows that the hedger is not able to cover conveniently.

How big should the pool of liquid assets be in order to provide adequate protection against adverse cash flows? This depends on the size of the futures position that is taken, the volatility of the futures price, and the anticipated length of the holding period. Another factor that can play a role is the length of the grace period that the FCM allows for a margin call to be met. One way to approach the problem is to estimate how far the futures price might move adversely to the futures position that has been taken within a given time period and to hold sufficient cash reserves to cover the margin calls that would result. For example, one might determine that if the pool of funds were exhausted, it would take one week to raise additional funds conveniently from another source (e.g., by liquidating long term bonds). In this case, the liquidity pool should contain enough funds to cover the largest variation margin call that would have a reasonable probability of developing over a period of five trading days.

One way to do this is simply to look at past history and to see how many times a price move of a given magnitude has occurred in the past over a comparable length of time. For example, suppose that a hedged position involved selling 125 Treasury bond futures contracts against a portfolio of long-term bonds. A futures price increase of one point on the T-bond contract would lead to a cash outflow from the futures account of $1,000 per contract, or a total of $125,000 on the position. To estimate the need for liquid assets to meet margin calls, one might look at historical data to find the largest price move that has occurred in this contract in the previous five years and hold sufficient funds to cover the margin call if that move should be duplicated. Coverage for a possible five-point move would involve a liquidity pool of $625,000.

A problem with this procedure is that price volatility can change over time, and past history may not be a sufficiently good gauge of the risk relevant to the present situation. Moreover, it is not necessarily optimal to hold a pool big enough to cover every price move that has occurred in the past. A more formal approach to the problem of choosing the correct liquidity pool would be to use data on the standard deviation of futures price changes to compute the probability of a price change of a given magnitude within a specified interval (or, equivalently, the size of the price change that has a given probability of occurring within the interval). This allows the hedger to base his decision about the size of the liquidity pool on an estimate of the actual risk he is facing, independent of whether a move of a given size has occurred in the past or not.

Suppose that the one day price change is normally distributed with a mean of zero and a standard deviation of σ. Assuming that the price moves are independent from one day to the next (an assumption which is widely supported by research), then the probability distribution of the price change over t days is

$$\text{Prob}(P_t < X) = N\left[\frac{X - P_0}{\sigma\sqrt{t}}\right]. \tag{7.1}$$

This expression gives the probability that the price in t days will be below some specific level X, given that it starts at price P_0. As before, $N[\cdot]$ denotes the standardized normal distribution function, which is tabulated and can be looked up in any statistics book. The probability that P_t will be above X is just 1.0 minus the probability it will be below X, as shown in equation (7.1).

Using this equation, one can easily estimate the probability of a t-day price move that would be large enough to exhaust a margin deposit of a given size.

Example: If σ is 0.70 per day, the probability of a price increase greater than 5.00 points in a five-day period is given by 1.0 minus the probability that the price will be less than 5.00 points higher.

$$1.0 - N\left[\frac{5.00}{0.70\sqrt{5}}\right] = 1.0 - N[3.19].$$

Looking this figure up in a table of the normal distribution gives the estimated probability of

$$1.0 - 0.99929 = 0.00071 = 0.71\%.$$

In Table 7-2 we show probability estimates for *percentage* price changes over time intervals ranging from one trading day to about three months (sixty trading days) for a variety of daily standard deviation figures. For example, if σ equals 15 percent, there is less than a 5 percent probability the price will increase by more than 4.84 percent in ten trading days.

Table 7–2.   Price Increase for which the Probability is less
than the Specified Value for Different Levels of Futures Price
Volatility and Hedge Horizon.

Prob-ability	σ	Length of Holding Period in Days					
		1	3	5	10	20	60
20%	5	0.26	0.45	0.58	0.82	1.16	2.02
	10	0.52	0.90	1.16	1.65	2.33	4.04
	15	0.78	1.35	1.75	2.47	3.49	6.05
	20	1.04	1.80	2.33	3.29	4.66	8.07
	25	1.30	2.26	2.91	4.12	5.82	10.09
	30	1.56	2.71	3.49	4.94	6.99	12.11
5%	5	0.51	0.88	1.14	1.61	2.28	3.95
	10	1.02	1.77	2.28	3.23	4.56	7.90
	15	1.53	2.65	3.42	4.84	6.84	11.85
	20	2.04	3.53	4.56	6.45	9.12	15.80
	25	2.55	4.42	5.70	8.07	11.41	19.76
	30	3.06	5.30	6.84	9.68	13.69	23.71
1%	5	0.72	1.25	1.62	2.28	3.23	5.60
	10	1.45	2.50	3.23	4.57	6.46	11.19
	15	2.17	3.75	4.85	6.85	9.69	16.79
	20	2.89	5.01	6.46	9.14	12.92	22.39
	25	3.61	6.26	8.08	11.42	16.16	27.98
	30	4.34	7.51	9.69	13.71	19.39	33.58

This table can be used in conjunction with an estimate of σ to estimate the probability of a price move large enough to cause inconve-
nience over a given time interval.[1] How large this probability ought
to be in a well-designed hedge program depends largely on the cost of
accessing other sources of funds if the liquidity pool should be exhausted, and the relative cost of tying up funds in liquid assets rather
than having them invested in less liquid securities at higher yields.

An important caution regarding this analysis is that the probability
distributions of futures prices have generally been found to be not exactly normal. There are more large price changes than expected from

---

1. To annualize a volatility figure estimated from daily data, multiply by $\sqrt{T}$ where $\sqrt{T}$ is
the number of trading days in a year, usually about 260.

a normal distribution. This means that probability estimates based on equation (7.1) will tend to underestimate the true probability of a big price move. Equation (7.1) should therefore be used conservatively, to obtain an estimate of the *minimum* probability of a given price move.

TRADING A FUTURES POSITION

In this section we will discuss some of the practical aspects of putting on a futures hedge, carrying it over time, and liquidating it either through offsetting the position in the futures market or by delivery.

Putting on a Hedge

The first step in putting on a hedge is obviously deciding what position should be taken. Since we have covered this issue in detail in earlier chapters, we will not linger on it here. The decision involves two different types of considerations, which interact with one another.

First, the hedger must decide how much of the risk he wishes to hedge. That is, given a set of risk-return possibilities that can be obtained using the available futures contracts at the current market prices, which is the preferred combination? Looking back to Figure 2–1, this is essentially the choice of which value of h to pick to achieve the preferred point along the risk-return possibility curve. There are several important things to think about in making this choice.

First, one should never use a hedge ratio that is high enough to push the position beyond the risk-minimizing h^*. Second, the choice of the optimal hedged position from among those on the positively sloped portion of the risk-return possibility curve depends on the hedger's risk tolerance — there is no unambiguously best position. One institutional investor, such as a stock trust account manager, might wish to bear all of the risk in his position in order to obtain all of the expected return, while another, such as a life insurance company making a commitment to purchase a private placement of debt, might wish to eliminate as much of the risk as possible during the commitment period. The decision of how much risk to bear can only be made by the manager.

Finally, the hedger will normally want to take into account whether the futures price is in line with its cost of carry level. If not, there is an extra return (or cost) to hedging available in the market. For example, if stock index futures are selling at a large premium above their theoretical value, a short hedger might want to take a relatively larger short position and a long hedger might want to reduce the size of his hedge.

In a similar vein, the price relationships in the cash market should be evaluated to see if the spread between the cheapest to deliver asset and the item being hedged is at an abnormal level. If so, and if the spread can be expected to move back toward the normal value during the hedge period, the profit or loss this will entail for the hedge will be an element to weigh in setting the hedge ratio.

The second type of consideration is precisely which contracts to trade and how to get into the market. One decision of this sort involves which futures market to trade in. As we discussed above, the choice will normally be to pick the contract which has maximum correlation with the price change on the cash position. The only exception to this rule might be in the case where the best futures market had limited liquidity and establishing a large enough futures position would affect the market price adversely. Another decision is which contract month to use. In most futures, the nearest to expiration month has the most liquidity, while the contract months more than two expirations out are sometimes difficult to trade in large size. For a long duration hedge, there is therefore a trade-off between matching the timing of the risk on the cash position versus trading the futures contracts in a liquid market. In such circumstances, most hedgers will find it more attractive to use the nearer contracts at first and to roll the hedge forward into the further months as these become more liquid.

Ideally, the hedger would like to know ahead of time what futures price he will trade at before taking on the cash position that he will be hedging. In some cases, it is possible to set the terms of the cash position, as when a commitment to buy securities at a fixed price or to guarantee a fixed rate of return is involved. In such cases, pricing the cash market position off the futures price and then hedging the position fixes the expected hedge return at a level that is known ahead of time.

Once a hedged position is established, it is necessary to monitor it regularly. Margin calls and marking to market are daily events and require frequent attention so that unpleasant surprises do not occur.

The hedge may need to be rebalanced periodically in order to maintain dollar equivalence as the prices in the marketplace fluctuate. Finally, the price relationship between the future and the item being hedged may change, which could alter the optimal hedge ratio. For example, if an unusually large short hedge was taken initially because the futures price was above its cost of carry level, the hedge ratio should be reduced when the price comes back into line. The monitoring that this involves is not very extensive or complex, but it is important to understand that a futures hedge should not simply be put on and left until it is time to liquidate the cash position.

Rolling over the Hedge

When a hedge is put on originally in a nearer contract month than the anticipated duration of the hedge, it will be necessary to roll the hedge forward at some point during its lifetime. This involves covering the position in the near future and reestablishing it in the more distant month. The procedure for doing this is not difficult, but it is important to do it in the correct manner.

It is risky to do the rollover in separate steps, since the cash position becomes temporarily uncovered in the process. For example, carrying the near futures position until it expires and then establishing a position in the more distant month the next day clearly exposes the position to risk, since the futures price can change adversely over night, before the hedge is reinstated. Even rolling the position over at a single point in time involves some risk. Depending on how big a position is involved, the risk due to minute-to-minute price volatility can be several ticks, enough to have a significant effect on the overall performance of the hedge, particularly when the roll has to be repeated several times over the lifetime of a hedged position.

A good way to avoid the rollover risk is to do the trade as a spread. This allows the hedger to cover the nearby futures contracts and reestablish the position in the more distant month simultaneously, at a price differential that is known ahead of time.

For example, suppose that on 5 March 1985 a life insurance portfolio manager had wanted to roll over a short position in one hundred March Treasury bond futures into the June contract. He would have found that the prices in the market were $69\frac{7}{32}$ for March delivery and $68\frac{7}{32}$ for June. He could do the roll by entering a spread order to buy one hundred March and sell one hundred June bond futures contracts at a spread of $^{32}/_{32}$. This would have eliminated the uncertainty involved in doing the transaction one leg at a time. Regardless of what prices the two transactions were executed at, the price difference would be fixed at $^{32}/_{32}$.

Moreover, since there was no fixed date on which the rollover had to be done, so long as it was completed before expiration of the near future, the spread order could be entered as an open limit order, to be executed at any time the prices were in the right configuration. This meant that the hedger had some leeway to wait for an attractive price differential before doing the transaction. For instance, in our example, a spread order might have been entered to buy March and sell June at a differential of $^{29}/_{32}$. If this was possible at any point, the rollover would be done at prices that were more favorable than anticipated by the amount of $^{3}/_{32}$. In fact, on 14 March, the two contracts closed at $69^{7}/_{32}$ and $68^{10}/_{32}$, so the spread could have been executed at the specified differential. Of course, one must not have unrealistic expectations about how much it is possible to gain by such a strategy. Attempting to trade the spread at a differential of, say, $^{25}/_{32}$ would have proved to be impossible, and the hedger would have found himself at the end of March forced to roll over at a price differential that was less attractive than what could have been obtained earlier.

What is an appropriate price differential for such a rollover? The answer comes from the cost of carry model, once again. In the same way that the theoretical futures price can be computed from the price of the cash market security by adding the net cost of carrying it until the futures expire, one can calculate the fair price differential between any two futures contract months as we described in Chapter 3.

The only added uncertainty has to do with the riskless interest rate that is used in the computation. It should be the rate that is expected to prevail over the time horizon under consideration. In our example, this would be the rate expected from the end of March up until the end of June. This is not difficult for the near future, but it could pose a problem for more distant expirations. One way to get an estimate of the rates for the relevant three-month periods as far as three years in the future is to look at the prices of matching Treasury bill futures contracts. It is even possible to hedge against adverse changes in the rate by trading the appropriate quantity of T-bill futures contracts, though for most cases this will not really be necessary.

Lifting a Hedge

Finally, let us consider the process of lifting the hedge. In nearly all cases this will be done by unwinding the futures position in the futures market and dealing separately with the cash market position.

As we have discussed earlier, hedge performance depends on the behavior of the basis during the hedging period. In many cases, the hedger will simply have to live with whatever the basis happens to be at the time that the hedge is to be lifted, even if that turns out to be unfavorable to him. For example, if the cash position being hedged is a portfolio of bonds held against a GIC that is maturing, there is no flexibility in unwinding the cash position, and there will be none in lifting the hedge either.

In other cases, however, there may be flexibility in the timing of lifting both parts of the hedged position. Suppose the futures contracts were purchased as an anticipatory hedge in order to lock in the yield for investing funds that were to become available at a particular future date. But suppose that when that date arrived, the basis was unfavorable for liquidating the position because the futures were selling below their theoretical level, given the prices currently available in the cash market. The hedger has the option of simply investing the funds in the short-term market and maintaining his futures position until prices become more favorable. There is no increase in risk in doing so, and the reversion of the basis to its correct value will lead to an increase in overall return on the hedge. (Naturally, the hedger must be right in his assessment of what the basis ought to be.) In some sense, this flexibility in lifting a hedge is like the option of choosing when to roll a futures position forward, but without the problem of a fixed deadline for the transaction.

The other option in lifting a hedge is making or taking delivery on the futures contracts. This is more or less feasible, depending on the particular future that is involved. In many cases the cash position being hedged cannot be delivered against the futures, as when T-bond futures are used to hedge a corporate bond position. Another problem is that of timing. Delivery, of course, is only possible on a particular date (or range of dates) so that it may not be possible at all to lift the hedge by delivery at the proper time. Finally, because the future will be priced to the cheapest to deliver security, it is generally not optimal to deliver the securities that are being hedged even when this is feasible.

Another feature of delivery is the existence of delivery options regarding what is to be delivered and when. Delivery options favor the short side of the futures market because it is up to the holder of the short position to choose how delivery is to take place within the permissible terms set by the contract. This means that a short hedger might reasonably elect to unwind his hedged position by delivering into the futures market, because he has control over the delivery process. A long hedger, on the other hand, might expose himself to considerable risk by taking delivery on his futures contracts. He cannot control which securities will be delivered, even though he knows that they are likely to be the cheapest deliverable, and in some cases he cannot even predict the delivery date with much certainty. The T-bond contract, for example, allows delivery on any business day during the delivery month.

For markets with cash settlement, notably the stock index futures contracts, going to delivery is substantially less risky than for other futures contracts because there are no delivery options. The only thing that can be delivered is cash, and the date is fixed. In this case, then, there is no real disadvantage to either side of the market, as long as the expiration date matches the desired date for lifting the hedge. The Treasury bill futures market also has a very "clean" delivery process. There is no uncertainty about what will be delivered, and the delivery date is fixed. However, other contracts, like Treasury bonds and especially GNMAs, contain several important and complex delivery options that make delivering optimally, and especially taking delivery, a tricky and hazardous procedure.

INDEX

ABOUT THE AUTHORS

Stephen Figlewski is Professor of Finance at New York University Graduate School of Business Administration, where he has taught since 1976. He holds a B.A. in Economics from Princeton and a Ph.D. in Economics from M.I.T. His teaching and research interests are largely in the field of financial markets. He has published extensively on futures and options markets, especially stock index futures, as well as in other areas relating to forecasting and speculative markets. Since 1983 he has been a member of the New York Futures Exchange and a Competitive Options Trader on the New York Stock Exchange, where he trades periodically on the floor as a market maker in stock index options and futures.

Kose John is an Associate Professor of Finance at the Graduate School of Business, New York University. He is currently a Visiting Associate Professor of Finance at the University of Chicago. He holds a Physics degree from Kerala University, India, and a Ph.D. in Business Administration from the University of Florida. He has won several awards for excellence in teaching and research. He has also won awards for paper presentations at professional meetings and has received several research grants. His publications are in the areas of options and futures markets, capital markets theory, and corporate finance.

John Merrick is an Assistant Professor of Finance at New York University Graduate School of Business, where he teaches courses on futures and options, and money, banking, and financial markets. He holds a Ph.D. in Economics from Brown University. His publications and research interests include work on futures and options markets, business cycles, and intertemporal asset pricing relations.

The Salomon Center

The Salomon Center for the Study of Financial Institutions is an endowment supported research center at New York University Graduate School of Business whose purpose is to support basic and applied research in finance and financial economics by leading academics and practitioners in the field. Partly due to its location in the heart of the New York financial district, the Salomon Center plays a unique role as an intellectual liaison between the academic and business communities.